Introduction to Show Networking

JOHN HUNTINGTON

ZIRCON DESIGNS PRESS

Copyright © 2020 by John Huntington, All Rights Reserved

No part of this book may be reprinted or reproduced or utilized in any form or by any electronic, mechanical, or other means, now known or hereafter invented, including photocopying and recording, or in any information storage or retrieval system, without permission in writing from the publisher.

Although every precaution has been taken to verify the accuracy of the information contained herein, the author and publisher assume no responsibility for any errors or omissions. No liability is assumed for damages that may result from the use of information contained within.

Trademark notice: Product or corporate names may be trademarks or registered trademarks, and are used only for identification and explanation without intent to infringe.

Zircon Designs Press

Brooklyn, NY, USA

www.zircondesigns.com

Print ISBN-13: 978-1-7357638-0-4

EBook ISBN-13: 978-1-7357638-1-1

LCCN: 2020918289

BISAC: Performing Arts / Theater / Stagecraft

Version 1.0, October 5, 2020

TABLE OF CONTENTS

PREFACE
What's Included and Not Included? xiv
For Whom Is This Book Written? xv
How Should This Book Be Used? xv
Conventions xvi
Disclaimers xvi
Thanks to My Production Team xvi
Website and Lecture Videos xvi

CHAPTER 1

INTRODUCTION
What Is a Network? 1
How are Networks Used on Shows? 1
    Lighting Networks 1
    Sound Networks 3
    Video Networks 3
    Scenery Networks 4
    Networks for Pyro, Costumes, Props, Show Control, You Name It! 5
Network Types 5
    Local Area Network (LAN) 6
    Wide Area Network (WAN) 6
    Internet 6
Networking Concepts 6
    Bit Rate/Bandwidth 6

Determinism. 7

Data Encoding 7

Error Detection 8

Packets and Frames 8

Packet Forwarding 8

Networking Using Electricity. 10

TIA Category Cables 10

Shielded or Unshielded Cables. 11

Solid or Stranded Conductors 11

RJ45 (8P8C) Connectors 11

TIA-568 Cabling Standard 12

Networking Using Light 14

Fiber Types. 14

Connectors 15

Networking Using Radio 15

Layering. 15

Open Systems Interconnect (OSI) Model 17

Here's Everything You Need To Know About Show Networking! 19

CHAPTER 2

ETHERNET

Logical Link Control (LLC) 22

Media Access Control (MAC). 22

CSMA/CD 22

MAC Address 22

Frame Check Sequence 23

Physical Layer (PHY) 23

Ethernet Implementations. 24

100Mbit/s 24

1 Gbit/s 24

2.5 and 5 Gbit/s 24

10 Gbit/s 24

Higher Rates 24

Ethernet Hardware 25

Network Interface Controller 25

Hubs 26

Switches 27

Routers 28

Media Converters and Bridges 29

Power over Ethernet (PoE) 29

IEEE 802.11 "Wi-Fi" 30

Basic Structure 31

Service Set IDentifier 31

Security Issues 31

Should You Use Wi-Fi On Your Show? 32

Why Ethernet is Good for Our Industry 33

CHAPTER 3

NETWORK OPERATIONS

Transmission Control Protocol (TCP) 36

User Datagram Protocol (UDP) 36

Internet Protocol (IP) 36

Address Classes 37

Broadcast Address 38

Loopback/Localhost IP Address 38

Private IP Addresses 38

Setting IP Addresses 39
    Dynamic Host Configuration Protocol (DHCP). 39
    Link-Local Addresses 40
    Static/Fixed IP Addresses. 41
Useful Commands Working with IP Addresses. 41
Subnets. 43
    A Simplified Subnet Mask Approach. 44
    Example Network with One Subnet 45
    Example Network with Two Subnets. 47
Address Resolution Protocol (ARP) 50
    ARP Command 52
Ports. 52
IPv6 53
    A New Address Format and Shorthand. 54
    Prefix/Subnet 55
    Three Types of Transmission 55
    Global Unicast 55
    Multicast 56
    Anycast. 56
    IPv6 Network Systems 56
    IPv6 in Show Networking? 56
Why IP Networking is Good For Our Industry 57

CHAPTER 4

MORE NETWORK OPERATIONS

Visualizing Traffic Flow. 59
Resolving Layer 2 and 3 Addresses 62
    Broadcast Domain 63

  Learning MAC Addresses 63

Network Topology Issues 64

  Broadcast Storms 65

  Managing Loops 67

  Virtual LANs (VLAN) 67

Routing 72

Other Network System Protocols 75

  Internet Group Management Protocol (IGMP) 75

  Domain Name System (DNS) 75

  Network Address Translation (NAT) 75

  Virtual Private Network (VPN) 76

  Quality of Service (QoS) 76

  Link Layer Discovery Protocol (LLDP) 76

Show Networking Best Practices 77

A Mature Solution 80

CHAPTER 5

EXAMPLE NETWORKS

Network Design/Implementation Process 83

  1: Analyze Network Needs 84

  2: Design Address/Subnet Scheme 84

  3: Determine Network Topology 84

  4: Document the Network 84

  5: Build, Label, and Verify the Network 85

  6: Implement Security 85

  7: Maximize Operational Reliability 86

Example Lighting Network 86

Example Sound Network 89

Example Video Network 93

Example Scenery Control Network 97

Example Managed Show Control Network 99

    Explaining The Network 107

CONCLUSION
Contact Info and Blog 113

APPENDIX: NUMBERING SYSTEMS
Base 10 (Decimal) Notation 115

Base 2 (Binary) Notation 116

Base 16 (Hexadecimal) Notation 117

Number Context 119

Converting Number Bases 119

Sample Numbers in Different Formats 122

INDEX
Index 125

PREFACE

This book reflects the impact of a dramatic, decades-long evolution in entertainment control technology[1], which started in the mid 1980s as digital control protocols replaced older analog approaches. Things developed rapidly from there, with networks first appearing in show systems in the mid 1990s. With the explosion of affordable computing and networking power, by the 2010s, mature networks were filling show-critical roles on all kinds of productions, and the field morphed from a bunch of individual, point-to-point connection methods to a variety of protocols and digital media data transported over a ubiquitous digital highway system: Ethernet.

This technological maturation led me to write the book you are reading, which traces its roots back to 1994, when the first edition of my *Control Systems for Live Entertainment* was published. That book (and its successors) covers the broad world of entertainment control (individual control systems as found in lighting, sound, video, machinery, pyro, lasers, etc.) and also show control (connecting two or more entertainment control systems together). I followed the market evolution over two more editions of that book over a couple decades, and then, reflecting the rise of the network, I reorganized the entire book for the self-published 2012 edition and changed the title to *Show Networks and Control Systems*. Five years later, I issued a second edition, and actually cut material out of the book because networks had become so dominant.

By design, and reflecting the realities of the market today, *Introduction to Show Networking* is smaller and less comprehensive than its predecessor. It is not meant to replace the larger book, but as networks have matured and been made easier to use by the brilliant engineers working for our manufacturers, many show technicians today will spend their career working on a mature hardware platform, and will be operating primarily at a higher virtual level. And at this level, they don't need to understand the low-level details that were so important in comprehending 1980s vintage control approaches. If you set things up right, use good-quality gear, and

---

[1] I developed a timeline wrote an article about this evolution for *Lighting and Sound America* that is available on my website, www.controlgeek.net.

follow some basic best practices, Ethernet *just works*. And since it's everywhere on shows, I hope this book will help technicians understand the basics of how it works; with the information here as a starting point, there are myriad resources available for the more advanced information, tailored to each usage.

WHAT'S INCLUDED AND NOT INCLUDED?

As the title *Introduction to Show Networking* suggests, this book is an introduction to the networks found on live shows: concerts, theatre productions, corporate and special events, cruise ship revues, wrestling shows, houses of worship, museum presentations, fountain spectaculars, etc.—any kind of show presented live for an audience. While we borrow and share technology with other forms of entertainment such as movies and television, those forms are not specifically included here. However, the basics of Ethernet are the same whether used in a concert or on a film set, so while the applications may be different, the core technologies covered here are the same. In addition, beyond a few examples, I don't focus a lot on specific usage by any particular show department, and this, too, is by design: a network is a network, and an IP address is an IP address, whether that IP address is used to transport streaming audio/video, lighting control data or pyro firing information.

This book focuses on understanding the basic technologies that allow data to be transported across a show network. By design, some complex operational protocols are introduced here but not explained fully, because while it's important for show techs to understand what some complex protocol offers us, and how to use it, they don't really need to know the gory details in order to use it effectively. However, if (like me) you find the low-level details intriguing out of curiosity (if not need), to try and get a low-level understanding of something like gigabit Ethernet or a modern network-based control or distribution protocol, you may need to develop some pretty advanced programming and engineering chops. I had a reasonably low-level understanding of the early versions of Ethernet, but even after learning about and teaching this stuff for more than 20 years now, I really have no low-level understanding about the electrical workings of gigabit Ethernet transmission. And that's because I don't really need to spend time learning that low-level, head-splitting detail in order to make a working, reliable system (my main interest).

And while I will mention the Internet here, and productions may (carefully) connect to it for either interactivity or maintenance, the complex operations of the larger Internet or corporate networks are also outside our scope here, and are well documented elsewhere (that said, I do have some thoughts about how to manage those connections—see "Show Networking Best Practices" on page 77). I don't specifically cover Internet streaming here, but again, the principles and best networking practices used on live shows can apply. I also don't discuss any specific gear or show software in this book; one reason for that is that the gear changes constantly, and in addition the specific ways that some networking features are implemented vary a lot by manufacturer. Finally, this book also does not include details on the control protocols that form so much of the basis of many entertainment control systems and much of the larger *Show Networks and Control Systems* book. That information remains available there and on many other sources, including my blog at www.controlgeek.net.

FOR WHOM IS THIS BOOK WRITTEN?

While not every entertainment technician needs to be a networking expert, I do believe that everyone working in entertainment technology should have at least a basic understanding of these critical technologies, since they are found on all kinds of shows in any department that uses technology. That said, this is a topic best approached by those who already have some experience in lighting, sound, video, scenery control, etc; it's easier to muddle through some of the arcane details here if you already are passionate about an area of our field. In addition, since I'm assuming most readers (like me) love building stuff more than they enjoy dealing with abstract information, I use a bottom-up approach, talking about cabling and the like before getting to the abstract layering concepts that traditionally are used to introduce networking technologies.

HOW SHOULD THIS BOOK BE USED?

I have attempted here to present the information in a form readable straight through by motivated, independent readers, while also making the structure modular enough to be useful for working professionals and educators (I teach classes based on the book myself).

To keep the applicability of the information here as broad as possible, if you see a computer represented in a diagram, imagine that could be anything on a show network: lighting console, network-enabled speaker, video server, pyro controller, etc.

You can do a lot in networking without understanding binary, but things like IP addresses are a lot easier to understand if you have a foundation in number bases. Since readers may or may not bring that knowledge, I've included an introduction in the "Appendix: Numbering Systems" on page 115.

CONVENTIONS

There are a number of cross references in this book. In print, they should refer to a page number; in electronic form they should take you to the related part of the book. However, I've only included forward cross references here when speaking about something we haven't covered yet. To look backward, there is a detailed Table of Contents and an Index.

If a term is **bolded**, then it is a "key" term; I generally mark the first major usage of the term in the book.

> Text in a box like this is an aside, historical or other information that is related to the topic in question but not part of the main flow.

DISCLAIMERS

And now for the *"It's not my fault!"* disclaimers: While I've made every effort to ensure that the information in this book is accurate, DO NOT implement anything in any product or system based solely on the information in this book. The goal here is understanding; if you want to go to the next level—*implementation*—you need to obtain information from the appropriate standards or other organizations. **Additionally, while networks can be used to control dangerous stuff, safety is the responsibility of system designers and operators.**

THANKS TO MY PRODUCTION TEAM

Literally hundreds of people helped me with this book and its predecessors over the years. But I want to extend a special thanks to Aaron Bollinger for creating all the excellent illustrations in the book; Shelbye Reese, who designed the fantastic layout and the cover, and Michael Lawrence for copy editing.

WEBSITE AND LECTURE VIDEOS

Errata for this book, my blog, and much more is available on my website: http://www.controlgeek.net. In addition, the site features lecture videos for chapters in the book:

Chapter 1

INTRODUCTION

WHAT IS A NETWORK?

A **network** is two or more devices using a common physical infrastructure to allow each connected computer to communicate with all the others. Any device connected by the network is called a **node**; if the node has data to communicate, it may be referred to as a **host**. **Ethernet,** the most widely-used network standard, offers incredible flexibility and power at a low cost, and—built correctly—Ethernet networks are robust, reliable and perform many mission-critical functions on our shows.

Networks are found on shows of all sizes, primarily serving two roles. First, networks transport control data to operate show equipment (lights, sound playback systems, video servers, automated scenery controllers, rigging controllers, pyro and special effect devices, etc.); this is a critical function they have been serving since the 1990s. Additionally, once network capacity increased, networks became widely used to transport, or "stream[1]", digital audio and video media. The real power of Ethernet is that—built correctly—the same network could work well in either role, carrying just about any kind of **digital** data for a show.

HOW ARE NETWORKS USED ON SHOWS?

Before moving on to details, let's take a look at how networks are used in various ways on shows, and introduce—at a high level—some realistic show networks, which we will revisit in detail at the end of the book. At this point, since we haven't covered any of the fundamentals, don't worry about how these systems work; instead focus on how they are structured and being used.

Lighting Networks

Lighting systems are all about control, and, traditionally, connections have been implemented with 1980s vintage point-to-point serial lighting control approaches

---

1 The term "streaming" is generally more associated with online Internet transport of media; we often operate on closed networks not connected to the larger Internet. More on this later.

like DMX512-A (Digital MultipleX) and RDM (Remote Device Management). As networking became cheaper and more powerful, network-based approaches to carrying lighting data such as Art-Net™, Streaming ACN (sACN, Architecture for Control Networks) and RDMnet became available[2]. Lighting networks can directly connect to controlled devices such as moving lights, dimmers, LED fixtures, and even fog machines and media servers. Or, the network might act as a backbone, transporting control data out to a "gateway", which converts it to older serial protocols like DMX512-A for direct, non-networked connections.

Example Lighting Network

This example lighting network for a simple system installed in a small venue is a mixture of both approaches, connecting a control console with several lights and a wireless remote phone app, and also transporting data to a gateway for traditional DMX control:

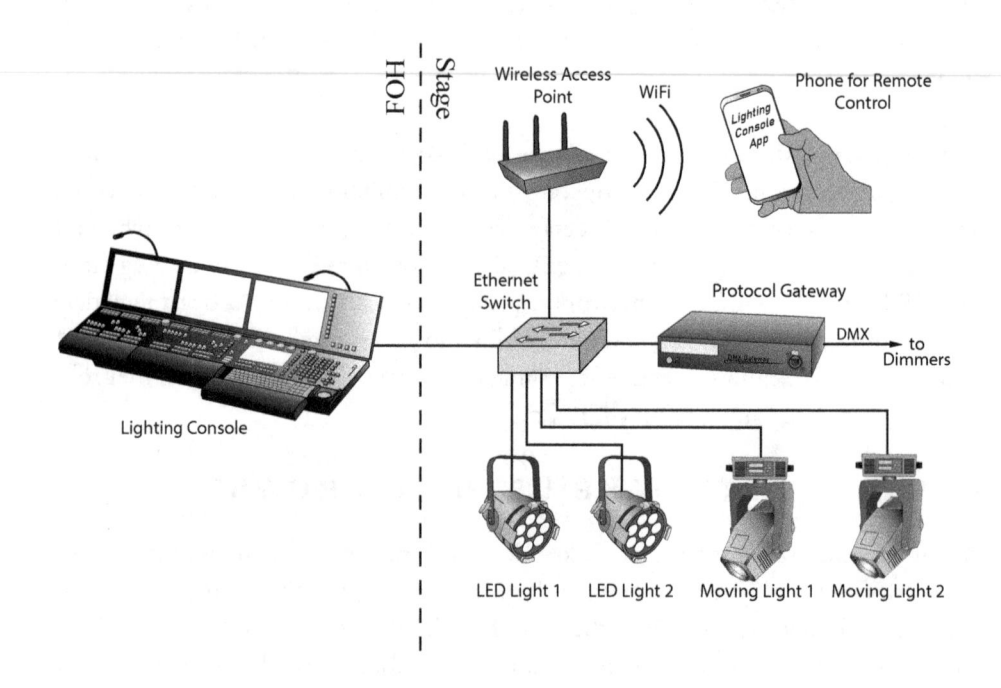

---

[2] Details on all of these and many more protocols and approaches can be found in my book, *Show Networks and Control Systems*.

• CHAPTER 1: INTRODUCTION

Sound Networks

As sound systems moved from analog to digital in the late 1990s, digital audio started to be transported over standard networking equipment, and this led to the eventual development of proprietary media networking approaches like Audinate's Dante®, or open approaches like AES-67 and the multi-named AVB (Audio Video Bridging) / TSN (Time-Sensitive Networking) / "Milan®". In addition, networks are used to transport a number of proprietary audio control systems implemented by manufacturers, as well as open control standards like OSC (Open Sound Control), MIDI (Musical Instrument Digital Interface) and AES-70 (Open Control Architecture).

Example Sound Network

In this example sound network for a one-off show, we share some networking hardware to transport two separate networks; one carries remote control data for the console; the other transports digital audio:

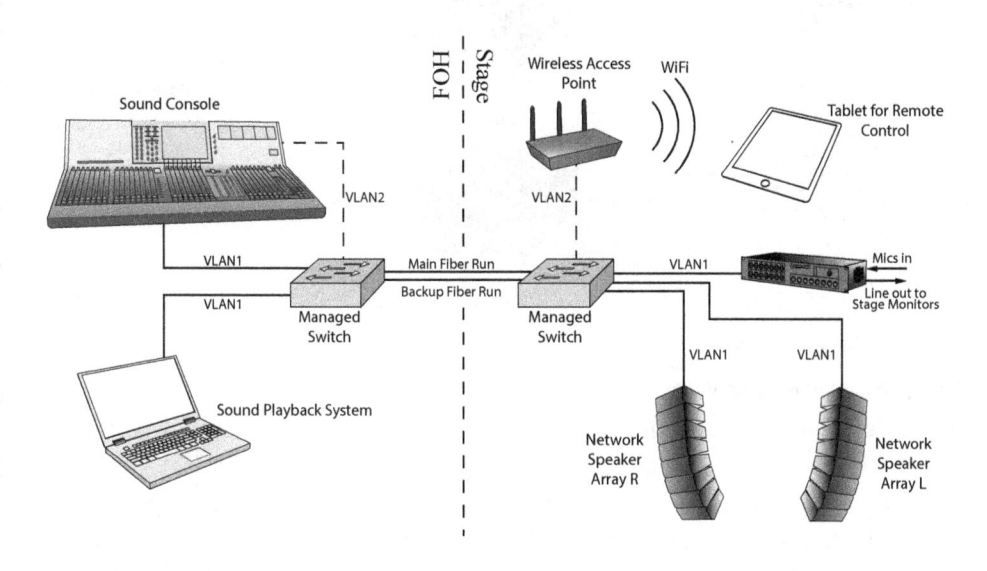

Video Networks

As computing power increased in the late 1990s, networks started being used widely as the control and distribution backbones of many video systems. And then in the 2010s, as affordable networks became capable of carrying and routing high-resolution digital video signals, open standards like SDVoE (Software Defined Video over Ethernet) and SMPTE 2110 were developed.

Example Video Network

This example video system for a permanent show in a museum is actually made up of two physically-separated networks: one for control and one for distribution of the high resolution video signals; some devices connect to both networks via separate physical connections.

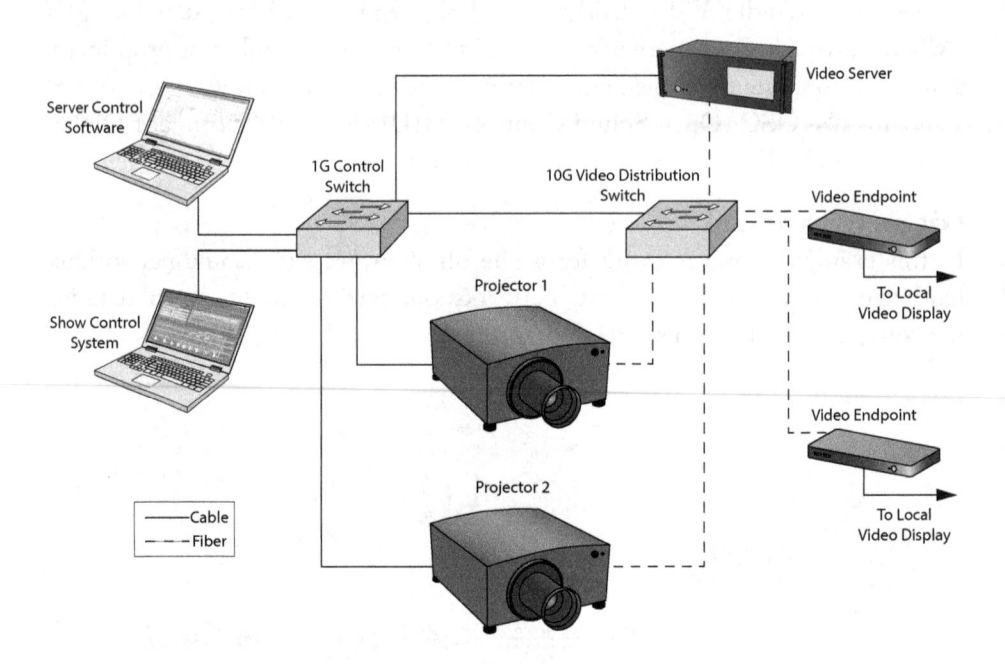

Scenery Networks

In scenic automation and rigging systems, networking started being used in the late 1990s to transmit control data between various controllers, input/output (IO) systems, and controlled devices; much of this is done via proprietary approaches from a single manufacturer, and this closed approach is often used to implement safety-rated connections. In addition, for simpler applications, protocols adapted from the days of serial, point-to-point connections like ModBusTCP are used. And as networks became ubiquitous, approaches to share positional data safely between systems, such as RTTrPM (Real-Time Tracking Protocol - Motion), became available.

Example Scenery Network

Scenic automation systems typically draw on the world of industrial controls, which, like the entertainment industry, builds on top of Ethernet as a backbone. This simple scenic automation system connects a controller, a remote pendant, a computer for display and editing of cues, and two drive units:

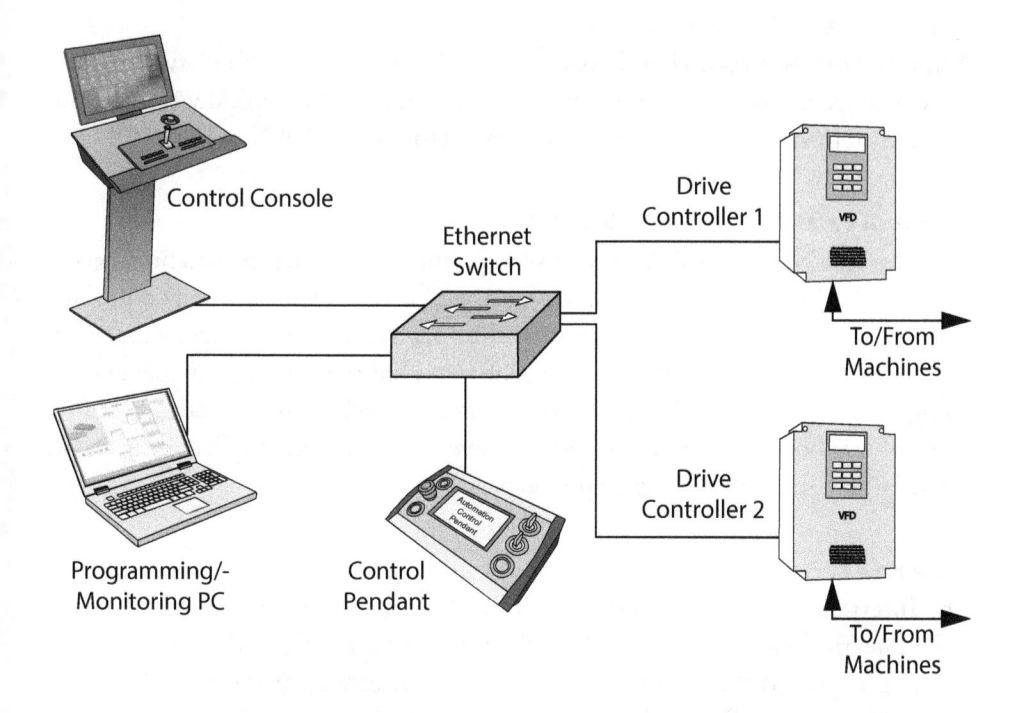

Networks for Pyro, Costumes, Props, Show Control, You Name It!

Networking presents such a powerful and affordable infrastructure that it is the obvious choice to carry just about any kind of digital data. You will find it in one form or another behind all kinds of systems throughout live shows. In addition, networks are ideal for **show control** applications, which connect together two or more **entertainment control systems** (lighting, sound, video, etc.), allowing the connected systems to synchronize or interact[3].

Keep these systems and applications in mind as we work through all the underlying details of networks; we will revisit, expand on and explain each of these example networks outlined above in the final chapter of this book (see the example systems on page 83).

NETWORK TYPES

We can break down networks into two basic types: Local Area Network (LAN) and Wide Area Network (WAN).

---

3 Much more on Show Control in my other book, *Show Networks and Control Systems*.

Local Area Network (LAN)

A **Local Area Network** (LAN) covers a "small area," ranging from two devices up to a single building or a small group of buildings, and is typically owned and maintained by one organization. Most show networks are LANs.

Wide Area Network (WAN)

A **Wide Area Network** (WAN) covers long distances, a wide area, or a broad geographic area. Of course, the best known usage of a WAN is to connect to the Internet. WANs typically use a "common carrier" such as a phone company for some or all of their connections and, therefore, are rarely entirely owned and operated by a single organization. WANs are a separate area of specialty, mostly outside of the scope of this book, and are rarely used for live entertainment applications except in the largest applications (e.g., a theme park).

Internet

The **Internet** is basically a network of networks. To the user, the Internet appears to be one giant network; but, in fact, the user's network, through their Internet service provider (ISP), is simply connected to many other private and public networks. The Internet Protocol (IP, page 36) is the basis of this system.

NETWORKING CONCEPTS

Before moving on to some practical concepts, let's go through some abstract, but important networking concepts.

Bit Rate/Bandwidth

A digital data link carries a binary[4] stream of 1s and 0s. The rate of transmission is known as the **bit rate**, which is measured in **bits per second** (bit/s, or BPS). Bit rate measurements use the International System of Units (SI) prefixes, so it's very common to see something like Mbit/s, a megabit (1 million) per second, or Gbit/s, a gigabit (1 billion) per second. Whatever the transmission medium, there is always some limit as to how much data a single communications connection can handle; this capacity is known as the channel's **bandwidth**. A "high bandwidth" connection can carry more than a "low bandwidth" link.

---

[4] See "Appendix: Numbering Systems" on page 115 for an explanation of binary.

Determinism

All networks have some transmission **latency** (delay), and in the wider Information Technology (IT) industry, if a web page is a bit slower to load today than it was yesterday it's an inconvenience. But in our industry, a delayed light cue could expose the workings of a magic trick, and ill-timed, stutter-y audio or video could ruin a live concert. So, the timely delivery of data as a critical need is one of the things that sets our industry apart from the larger business networking world, and it drives the way we design and configure our networks. Data communications systems that can deliver data in a predictable amount of time are said to be **deterministic**. Actually guaranteeing a delivery time can involve complex systems; in many cases, "good enough" delivery time is more than adequate for the task, especially when we are sending relatively small amounts of data over systems with a very large available bandwidth.

Data Encoding

To allow systems to communicate over a network, we must first agree on the way that machines model and represent the physical world, and make sure that all devices communicating with one another use an agreed-upon approach. For specific kinds of data like audio samples, "Light Cue 13 Go," or "platform move at 66% speed," there are specific standards[5]. However, deserving a mention here are three interrelated, open data character encoding standards prevalent in the world of networking: the **American Standard Code for Information Interchange** (ASCII), **Unicode**, and the Universal Character Set's (UCS) widely used **UTF-8** variant.

ASCII (pronounced ASS-kee) was standardized in the early 1960s, and is basically a grown-up version of a communication game you may have played as a child: substituting numbers for letters of the alphabet in order to send coded messages. For example, to send the text "Ethernet" in ASCII, the following decimal and hex[6] numbers would be used:

Character	E	t	h	e	r	n	e	t
Decimal	69	116	104	101	114	110	101	116
Hex	45	74	68	65	72	6E	65	74

---

5 And many of these are covered in my other book, *Show Networks and Control Systems*.

6 See "Appendix: Numbering Systems" on page 115 for an explanation of hexadecimal numbers.

ASCII was, and UTF-8 is now, one of the most widely-used standards in computing and networking, and many other standards reference or use them. UTF-8 and Unicode are backwards compatible, and in basic control systems we're likely to be using pretty simple characters, so most people call just this standard "ASCII"[7].

Error Detection

No communications link is perfect; there is always some possibility of an error occurring in the transmission—whether caused by noisy lighting dimmers or a loose connector. **Error detection** schemes add some data to the information traveling over the link, and offer the receiver a mechanism to determine if the data was corrupted during transmission (or storage). The **Cyclic Redundancy Check** (CRC) approach, which is included in Ethernet, is an extremely effective error-detection method, with accuracy approaching 100% in many implementations. Basically, with the CRC approach, the data to be checked is treated as a block of bits, which is divided using a specially designed polynomial. The result of the division is transmitted along with the data for verification by the receiver. If the receiver detects some corruption, it can request for the data to be resent, or discard it.

PACKETS AND FRAMES

In "old school" analog or point-to-point digital connections, a continuous, physical data communications pathway exists between two (or a few) communicating devices, which simply sends voltages representing information back and forth. Networks, on the other hand, share a common physical infrastructure to create virtual connections, so the data traffic must be managed, or packaged, in some way. The most typical approach is to break the data up into **packets** or **frames** with each unit containing a small chunk of the larger data stream. (Whether a data unit is called a packet or a frame depends basically on what layer it occupies; more on that shortly on page 15). The packetized nature of networks adds another level of complexity, since it's possible for packets to arrive at the receiving node delayed, out of order, or corrupted. Higher-level protocols are required to handle these issues, but the benefits of flexibility and sophisticated cross-system interoperability far outweigh the drawbacks.

Packet Forwarding

Packets on a network can be delivered in different ways, depending on the application, and the network components can make a decision on a packet-by-packet

---

[7] There are many websites available that show the ASCII characters and related numbers.

basis whether to forward (or not) a packet to a particular interface. The three basic delivery types we will cover are unicast, multicast, and broadcast. The different approaches can each have a place in a network, depending on what is needed, and networks can operate in different modes at different times, broadcasting data at some times, multicasting at others, and then unicasting as well.

Unicast

Unicast delivery simply means that packets from one sender are forwarded through a network to a single destination.

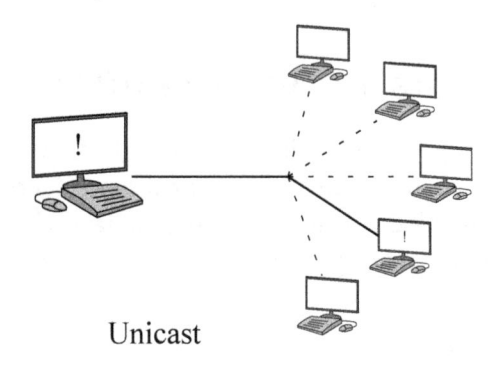

Unicast

Multicast

When data is forwarded from one transmitter to two or more receivers simultaneously, this is called **multicasting**. Multicast communications on a network maximize efficiency by allowing the sender to send a particular packet of data only once, even though the data is delivered to multiple receivers.

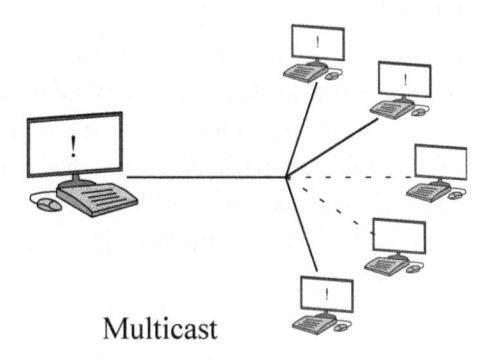

Multicast

Broadcast

Broadcast delivery is where data is sent to every single connected device (or network segment, see "Broadcast Domain" on page 63). This approach is very simple and effective. On the other hand, broadcasting is inefficient, since every packet uses network bandwidth and receivers that don't need the data still have to deal with it.

Broadcast

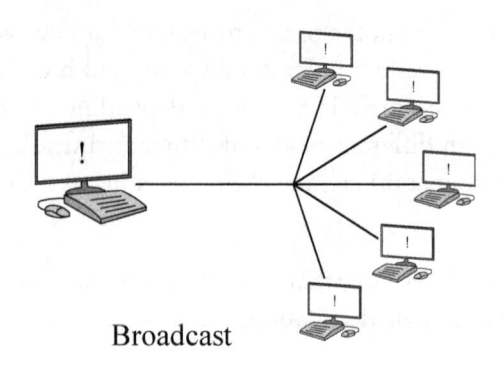

NETWORKING USING ELECTRICITY

The most common physical networking method is the transmission of electricity over wires, with the state of the circuit's electrical signal representing (and communicating) the 1's and 0's that make up the digital data. This approach is cheap, reliable, well understood, and easy to install and troubleshoot.

TIA Category Cables

Networks transmit at high transmission rates, and the construction and installation of the cable is a critical part of the networking system. Cables for networking are grouped into "categories" generally standardized by the Telecommunications Industry Association (TIA).

Category 5e

Category 5e or "**Cat 5e**" cable[8] is widely used. While the "e" in Cat 5e cable indicates some enhancements over the older and now obsolete Category 5 cables, the cables are sometimes just referred to as "Cat 5". First standardized in 2001, Cat 5e allows 100 meter runs of Ethernet speeds up to 1 Gbit/s (with some higher rate, special uses possible). With 1 Gbit/s capacity, Cat 5e offers enough bandwidth for all but the most demanding show networking applications. And while typical Cat 5e cable is very difficult to coil for show purposes, show-oriented cable versions are available.

Category 6

Category 6 is backwards compatible with Cat 5/5e, and designed to handle 1 Gbit/s and shorter runs of 10 Gbit/s.

---

8 Before Cat 5e came to rule the networking world, there were categories 1-4, ranging from old "plain old telephone service" or "POTS." up through Cat 5, which was similar to 5e but had some electrical issues with "crosstalk".

10 • CHAPTER 1: INTRODUCTION

Category 6A
Category 6A is backwards compatible with Cat 6, and features more stringent cable construction requirements, can run 10 Gbit/s Ethernet at 100m distances.

Category 7/8/etc.
Cable construction is an ever-escalating race, and with Cat 7 and above, it's getting so application specific that you are not likely to encounter it on most show networking applications. If you're needing these levels of bandwidth, you should contact the manufacturer of the gear you are connecting and see what they recommend. But also keep in mind that some of these super high bandwidth connection methods may be overkill and can create additional complexity if you're not in need of the features. Cat 5e is just fine for many types of networking.

Shielded or Unshielded Cables
Twisted pair cable,[9] made of pairs of two wires twisted tightly together, works especially well with the kind of differential, balanced transmission used for noise rejection in high-speed digital transmission. This type of twisted pair cable, without a shield, is called **Unshielded, Twisted Pair** (UTP). UTP is cheap, effective, and easy to install, and is used in many networks. Adding a shield to the cable—such as metal foil or a braid of tiny conductors—can offer additional resistance to electrical noise, and also reduce the amount of noise emitted from the cable. This type of cable is known as **Shielded, Twisted Pair** (STP).

Solid or Stranded Conductors
Networking cable is available with either **solid** or **stranded** conductors. Solid conductors are easier to terminate in jacks and generally lose less signal; of course they also make cables nearly impossible to coil (and repeated flexing of solid conductors can cause them to break). For these reasons, solid cables are generally used for permanent installation, while stranded cables are used for temporary patch and connection cables.

RJ45 (8P8C) Connectors
Networks mostly use the connector shown, which is an **8P8C** (eight positions, eight conductors), but is more widely (although technically incorrectly) referred to as an **RJ45**, available both in plug and jack form. RJ stands for "registered jack," and the RJ series connector, which was developed by the telecommunications industry, specifies both the connector *and* the wiring configuration. The 45 variation was originally designed as an 8-position connector carrying (in some applications)

---

9 Twisted pair cable was actually patented by Alexander Graham Bell in 1881.

only a single pair of wires, but it looks very similar to the 8P8C connector specified for Ethernet. The actual telecom RJ45 connectors and configuration are now obsolete, but the 8P8Cs are almost universally referred to as RJ45s. Because of this, I will refer to these connectors as RJ45 (8P8C) throughout this book.

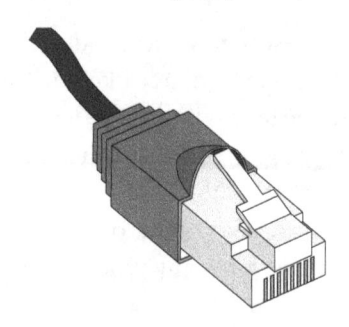

The RJ45 (8P8C) has eight pins and can connect four pairs of wire. RJ45 (8P8C) connectors are made of easily-shattered plastic, and are not well suited to the backstage environment. However, they are extremely inexpensive and can be easily installed in a few seconds with "crimping" tools. Some available varieties of these connectors have small ramps on either side of the release tab, protecting them when a cable is pulled through a tangle. In addition, the industrialized Ethercon® connector from Neutrik and other similar connectors are available for our heavy-duty applications.

TIA-568 Cabling Standard

The TIA-568 standard specifies a "structured" layout of network wiring for a building. The standard is very complex, but basically it takes a typical multistory office building and breaks its cable infrastructure into "vertical" and "horizontal" runs. Vertical cables are high-bandwidth "backbones," which connect through network distribution systems to a floor's individual "horizontal" lines (limited to runs totaling 100 meters or less). The horizontal cables are sometimes run through air-handling plenums, so a type of cable for this application is often called "plenum" cable. The vertical cables may run through cable risers in buildings, and because they run vertically, "riser" cables must have a high fire resistance rating. Installing a permanent network-based cable system is not something that a casual user should attempt without some research and experience; and of course there are capable contractors who also have the test equipment needed to certify the installation. Further details of the 568 standard are outside the scope of this book, but there is one important aspect you may encounter: the pin designations in the standard.

T568A and T568B for RJ45 (8P8C) Connectors

The wire pair and color code pinout on RJ45 (8P8C) connectors is perhaps the best-known aspect of the 568 cabling standard, and also is perhaps the most confusing. The 568 standard designated two pin outs for RJ45 (8P8C) connectors: one called **T568A**, and the other called **T568B**. On the RJ45 (8P8C) plug, the pins lay out as shown in the graphic.

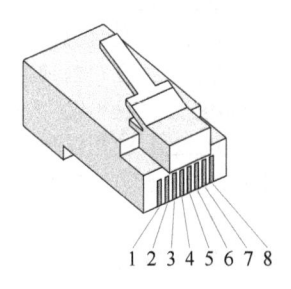

Cat 5e cable is the most widely used cable with this sort of connector, and has four tightly twisted pairs of wires. To accommodate fast network speeds, the physical configuration of the wire pairs is critical, and this explains the seemingly strange pinout specified in T568A and B.

The first pair of wires is in the center of this family of connectors (to give some backwards compatibility to pair 1 on RJ11 and similar connections). The second pair splits across the first, and then both wires of pairs 3 and 4 are adjacent and out toward the edges of the connector (they could not continue the splitting scheme further due to crosstalk and other issues). The only real difference between the T568A and T568B schemes is that two pairs are swapped; so, if you are wiring a facility, it really doesn't matter (functionally) whether you use A or B, as long as you use the same standard on both ends of every cable. The vast majority of entertainment applications use the T568B pin out:

Pin	T568B Pair	Wire	T568B Color
1	2	Tip	White with orange stripe
2	2	Ring	Orange solid
3	3	Tip	White with green stripe
4	1	Ring	Blue solid
5	1	Tip	White with blue stripe
6	3	Ring	Green solid
7	4	Tip	White with brown stripe
8	4	Ring	Brown solid

Here is the standard for the less common "A" pin out:

Pin	T568A Pair	Wire	T568A Color
1	3	Tip	White with green stripe
2	3	Ring	Green solid
3	2	Tip	White with orange stripe
4	1	Ring	Blue solid
5	1	Tip	White with blue stripe
6	2	Ring	Orange solid
7	4	Tip	White with brown stripe
8	4	Ring	Brown solid

NETWORKING USING LIGHT

Instead of sending electrons over wire to send data, it is possible to turn on and off a light source to represent the data bits being transmitted.

Fiber Types

While it's possible to send data using light through the air, it is typically more useful in show networking applications to send light through a glass or plastic optical fiber. Light travels down a length of this **fiber-optic cable** by bouncing back and forth off the boundary edge between the center glass or plastic and the air, or between the center and a jacket known as the cladding, or buffer.

Fiber comes in two types: multi-mode and single-mode. Multi-mode allows multiple "modes," or pathways, for the light to bounce. Single-mode allows fewer possible pathways for the light beam, which leads to fewer bounces, which in turn leads to less loss. These characteristics allow extremely high bandwidth, but single-mode fiber is more difficult to terminate, needs more accurate end alignment, and is therefore more expensive to use.

Because fiber carries only light, fiber-optic data links are completely immune to electrical interference. Potential bandwidth in fiber is extremely high, but this high bandwidth and noise immunity comes at a price: Compared to wire, fiber-optic cable is more expensive and more difficult to terminate. So, while fiber has become more common in our industry, it's still usually installed only when high bandwidth, very long cable runs, or extreme noise immunity is required.

Connectors

A variety of fiber connectors exist; in the 2020s, the most common fiber connector in our industry has been the LC type. LC-Duplex is a pair of LC connectors.

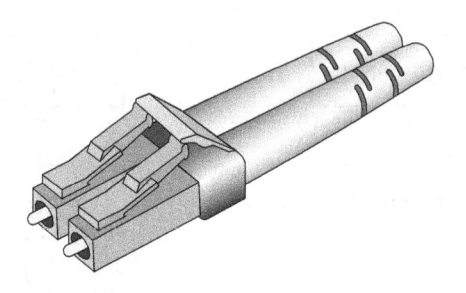

Small Form-Factor Pluggable (SFP) Interfaces

Fiber is often used to connect networking equipment together, and flexible Small Form-factor Pluggable (SFP) interfaces allow either copper or fiber connections directly to equipment. For some high bandwidth applications, SFP and higher rate SFP+ connections can also be used directly.

NETWORKING USING RADIO

The third way to transmit data is to use radio signals to encode the 1's and 0's of the data. The most common radio data transmission we are likely to encounter is IEEE 802.11 "Wi-Fi," which is covered on page 30. Also, there are some commercial approaches to transmitting DMX over a spread spectrum signal (see "Wireless DMX Transmission," on page 239). However, because of the potential for radio interference and many failure modes, RF links are rarely as robust as wire or fiber-optic links, so I still advise using copper or fiber if at all possible and radio of any variety only when there is no other practical option.

LAYERING

Let's bring this all together by taking a step back, and look at the process of network communication through a wider lens. Many older standards commonly used in the entertainment industry specify the details of everything needed to establish communications: the physical connections (voltages, connectors, interfaces, etc.), data transmission details, and the commands ("Go") or data format. Control and distribution standards developed in the era of the network, however, generally only specify the higher-level details, and leave details of transmission to independent, underlying technologies.

Key to this approach is a concept called "**layer**ing." In a layered communications system, the communication tasks are broken down into component parts. Let's imagine a network modeled using a simple, hypothetical three-layer system, with the layers called "Application," "Transport," and "Physical."

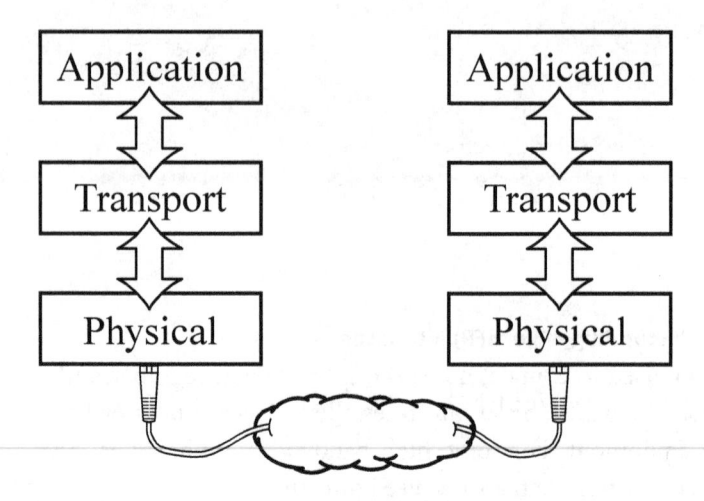

The Application layer contains the system processes that interface with the user or control or media system; Transport ensures that the messages get from one place to another, while keeping them intact and in order; and Physical specifies the interface type, the type of connectors, bit rate and other similar details. With this layered control approach, the data passed to other layers is typically **encapsulated** into another protocol, with additional information added as a "wrapper", including things like protocol type, source and destination addresses, etc.

The tasks of each layer are compartmentalized and independent, since each layer only needs to know how to talk with the layer above it and the layer below. For example, the Application layer really doesn't care about the details of how its messages get from one machine to another; it simply has to receive its data from the user and then present it to the Transport layer (and vice-versa, of course). The transport layer doesn't know anything about the actual connectors, and it doesn't make any difference if the signal is traveling over a wired or wireless link or a fiber-optic cable. It simply needs to know how to talk to the Physical layer, which takes care of all those details. In addition, this layered approach gives us modularity; if we want to change one layer we can leave the rest intact. And protocols and approaches developed using this scheme allow us to easily build on other, widely used, standardized building blocks, saving us time and simplifying the entire process.

Open Systems Interconnect (OSI) Model

With the basic concept of layering introduced, let's look in more detail at the most widely used approach, the **Open Systems Interconnection (OSI) model**. The OSI model consists of seven discrete layers, each performing one part of the communications and networking task, building on the services offered by the next lowest layer. The approach is complex and represents an idealized model; some network systems combine or leave out layers altogether and do not strictly follow the model. However, OSI is a helpful tool for understanding the functions of networks, and you may hear its terminology used in descriptions of network hardware and design, so a brief description is included here.

Through OSI, a layer in one device can effectively communicate with its counterpart layer in another device on the network, even though the only actual physical connection between the two devices is the physical layer.

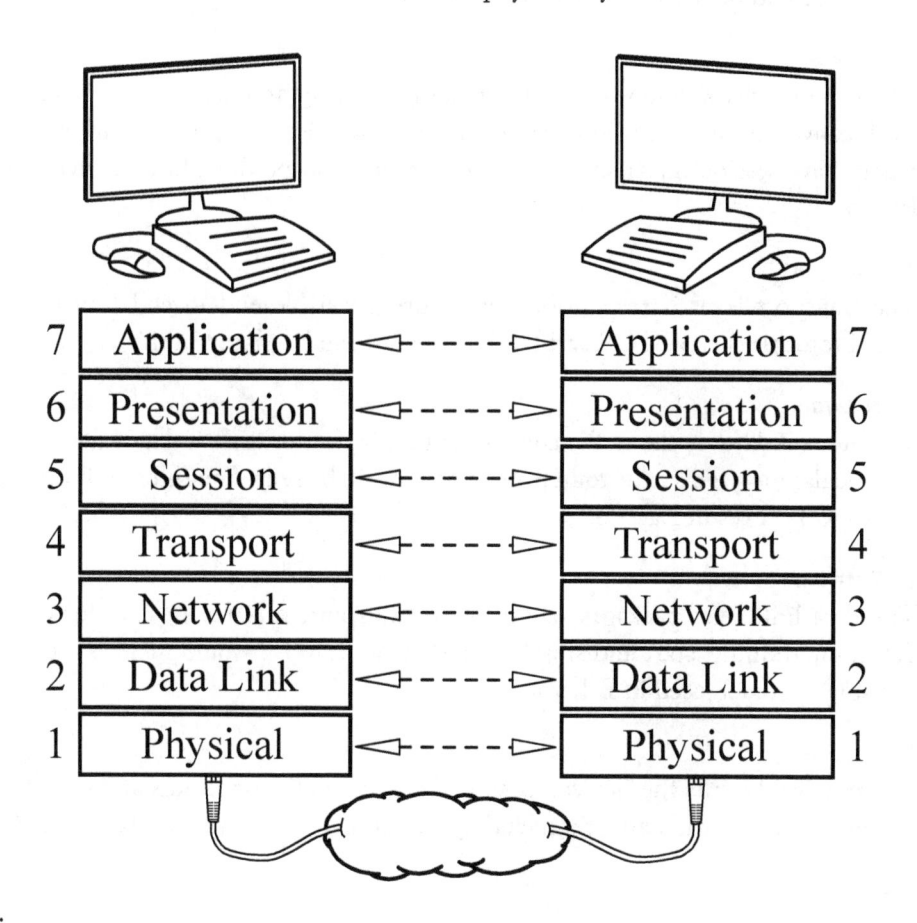

7	Application	<---->	Application	7
6	Presentation	<---->	Presentation	6
5	Session	<---->	Session	5
4	Transport	<---->	Transport	4
3	Network	<---->	Network	3
2	Data Link	<---->	Data Link	2
1	Physical	<---->	Physical	1

OSI is incredibly powerful but can also be confusing—it is often difficult to discern separate functions for some of the layers, especially the ones near the middle. Fortunately, as end users, we are generally able to leave this task to our equipment manufacturers and protocol designers, but it is important to understand the concepts, so a brief introduction to each of the OSI layers is offered here.[10]

7—Application
The application layer, the "highest" layer in OSI, is where the meaning of data resides, and this layer presents resources for applications programs run by users. A web browser, for example, can be thought of as occupying this layer.

6—Presentation
The presentation layer is responsible for presenting the raw data to the application layer; file and data transformation and translation are the responsibility of this layer, allowing different applications to access the same network. Encryption, for example, could be placed in this layer of the model.

5—Session
The session layer is responsible for managing and synchronizing the overall network conversation, or "session." Some of the more advanced protocols in our industry have session management protocols that could be thought of as living in layer 5.

4—Transport
The transport layer is responsible for ensuring reliable end-to-end transfer of data. Protocols such as TCP and UDP (page 36) can be placed in this layer.

3—Network
The network layer is the traffic control center for the network; it determines how a particular message can be routed and where it will be sent. The Internet Protocol (IP, page 36) lives in Layer 3.

2—Data Link
The data link layer packages raw data for transport; it is responsible for error detection, framing, start and stop bits, and so on. Layer 2 would include the addressing approach used in Ethernet.

1—Physical
The physical layer is the "lowest" layer of OSI, and defines the nuts and bolts (or bits and volts) of the network, including bit timing, data rate, interface voltage,

---

10 One mnemonic I learned in Cisco CCNA bootcamp that helps me remember the layer names and order, starting at the bottom (physical) layer is, "Please Do Not Throw Sausage Pizza Away" (Physical-Data-Network-Transport-Session-Presentation-Application)

mark and space values, connectors, and so on. The physical layer has no intelligence about what kind of data is being sent; data is simply treated as raw bits.

HERE'S EVERYTHING YOU NEED TO KNOW ABOUT SHOW NETWORKING!

OK I'm joking here, but with the introductory networking concepts in place, let's lay out in a few bullet points the key things an entertainment technician needs to build and operate the majority of show networks:

- Use appropriate hardware (see Chapter 2, "Ethernet" on page 21).
- Every machine on the network needs a unique and appropriate IP address (manually or automatically assigned) and Subnet Mask (see Chapter 3, "Network Operations" on page 35).
- Keep your cable runs under 100 meters and do not make loops in your network topology (unless managed) and follow best practices (see Chapter 4, "More Network Operations" on page 59).
- Methodically follow a best-practices-based design, implementation, and documentation process (see Chapter 5, "Example Networks" on page 83).

Chapter 2

ETHERNET

You will find **Ethernet** on shows of all sizes, acting as our default digital highway system. It carries lighting control data, connects video control equipment, links show control computers to sensing systems, transports multichannel digital audio and video, connects components in scenic motion-control systems—you name it. If it's digital data, Ethernet is carrying it for us.

Ethernet's development began in the 1970s to enable users at their "workstations," then a radical concept, to transfer files using a network. In 1983, Ethernet was first standardized under the auspices of the Institute of Electrical and Electronic Engineers (IEEE), and the **IEEE 802.3** Ethernet Working Group is still very actively developing extensions and new systems (and the 802.11 group works on wireless Ethernet technologies). IEEE 802 is such an unwieldy mouthful—and few people use the formal name anyway—so I will refer to it in this book simply as Ethernet.

Ethernet is responsible only for transporting bits from one place or another, while higher-level protocols (such as TCP, IP, ARP, see "Network Operations" on page 35) are responsible for packaging the data and making sure that the message is delivered reliably and appropriately. Ethernet breaks down into three general layers (from top to bottom): Logical Link Control (LLC), Media Access Control (MAC), and Physical (PHY). LLC and MAC can be thought of as co-occupying OSI Layer 2, Data Link, while the Ethernet PHY layer fits into OSI Layer 1, Physical.

OSI	Ethernet Layer
Upper Layers	Not Ethernet: TCP, UDP, IP, HTTP, DHCP, FTP, etc. and many entertainment control and media protocols
Layer 2: Data Link	Logical Link Control (LLC)
	Media Access Control (MAC)
Layer 1: Physical	Physical (PHY)

Let's go through each Ethernet layer.

LOGICAL LINK CONTROL (LLC)

The **LLC layer** receives data packaged by an upper-level protocol and passes it on to the MAC layer for transmission onto the network (of course, data also flows in the other direction upon return).

MEDIA ACCESS CONTROL (MAC)

The **MAC layer** connects the LLC layer (and, therefore, everything above it) and the physical Ethernet media in the PHY layer below. There are three aspects of the MAC layer that are useful to understand, so I will introduce here CSMA/CD, the MAC Address, and the Frame Check Sequence (FCS).

CSMA/CD

The Carrier Sense, Multiple Access (CSMA) approach was one of the foundation technologies that made Ethernet work and become popular; while we rarely use these techniques for wired Ethernet anymore, a brief historical overview of the technology is warranted. In early Ethernet implementations using CSMA, the network media was shared, all the nodes in the network had equal access (hence "multiple access"), and all nodes could hear everything and know whether or not another node was transmitting ("carrier sense"). If the network was found to be busy, the node would wait until the link cleared, and then transmit its data. The problem came when two nodes started sending at the same time. You have probably experienced this in a group conversation, where two people start talking at the same time; humans can hear this problem occurring and one or more of the talkers can "back off". But computers need a mechanism to handle this "data collision," and this is where the final part of the acronym came in: "Collision Detection" (CD). After a collision was detected, to ensure equal access, nodes waited a random amount of time before attempting to transmit again (if the retry time was fixed, nodes with shorter retry times could dominate the network). With the advent of full-duplex switches (page 26) CSMA/CD is no longer needed for wired networking, and we were happy to remove the random time element from our wired applications. With the shared media of radio, however, radio-based approaches (page 15) often still use a CSMA/CD approach.

MAC Address

Just like houses on a street, every node on a network needs a unique address so frames can be delivered properly. In Ethernet, each frame includes both the source and destination "physical" address, which is a globally unique 48-bit[1] **MAC address**, named after this Media Access Control layer, and burned into an Ethernet Network Interface Controller (NIC, page 25) at the factory, or otherwise stored in nonvolatile system memory. MAC address conflicts are avoided through the use of the Organizationally Unique Identifier (OUI), a 24-bit number used as part of the MAC address, with ranges of addresses purchased in blocks by Ethernet interface manufacturers from the IEEE. As long as the manufacturer ensures that they don't put the same OUI into more than one device, this scheme creates globally unique MAC addresses.

Frame Check Sequence

The **frame check sequence** (FCS) occupies the final 32 bits of the Ethernet MAC frame, and is a CRC check of all the bits in the frame, except the preamble, the start frame delimiter, and the FCS itself. This error detection is one of the important benefits of Ethernet for our purposes—every single frame includes a powerful error check.

This all makes for an Ethernet frame that lays out like this (simplified version for clarity):

Preamble	MAC Destination Address	MAC Source Address	Data Payload	Frame Check Sequence (CRC)

PHYSICAL LAYER (PHY)

The **Physical layer** (PHY) details the lowest levels of the system: the hardware. While there are many flavors of Ethernet, all the copper-based standards mandate the use of transformers to couple to the cable, which results in electrical isolation of around 1500V (depending on the type). Isolation, of course, is something we always want on shows, since we are often connecting low voltage computers to high-voltage devices; this is yet another benefit of Ethernet for our purposes.

There are a wide variety of Ethernet types, originally notated by a data rate in Mbit/s, signaling method and an indicator of physical media type. So for example, "100BASE-TX" means 100 Mbit/s data transmission rate and baseband trans-

---

1 Binary is covered in "Appendix: Numbering Systems" on page 115

mission over Cat 5 (or above) cable. As the standards evolved, the names have evolved and it's more typical now to just refer to an Ethernet version by the speed.

ETHERNET IMPLEMENTATIONS

Let's look at a few types of Ethernet common in show networks.

100Mbit/s

100BASE-T, introduced in 1995 and also referred to as "Fast Ethernet," runs at a data rate of 100 Mbit/s, using one pair of a Cat 5e UTP or STP cable for transmission and another pair for reception. RJ45 (8P8C) connectors are used, and the maximum segment length is specified at 100 meters; for longer runs, fiber variants are also available. As of this writing in 2020, this older standard is only found in lower end devices that don't need the faster Gigabit speeds.

1 Gbit/s

1000BASE-T, or Gigabit Ethernet (also known as GbE or 1 GigE), offers 1,000 Mbit/s and was published by the IEEE in 1999. It uses all four pairs of Cat 5e or better cable using RJ45 (8P8C) connectors and is the most common Ethernet variant used in the early 2020s. Cat 5e run lengths are limited to 100m; for longer runs, fiber versions are available.

2.5 and 5 Gbit/s

2.5GBASE-T and **5GBASE-T** run at T 2.5 Gbit/s and 5 Gbit/s, and use some technology from the faster 10 Gbit/s (see below), but allow 100 meter runs on Cat 5e (2.5 Gbit/s) and Cat 6 (5 Gbit/s) cable.

10 Gbit/s

10 Gigabit Ethernet (also referred to as 10GE, 10GbE, or 10 GigE) carries 10 gigabits per second for very high-bandwidth applications like high resolution video and backbones for heavy traffic. Given the blinding speeds, this standard typically runs over Cat 6 and higher cable or fiber, with run lengths varying by the connection method. Be sure to research your application carefully before determining the appropriate physical connection type.

Higher Rates

Ethernet is under continuous development by IEEE, and higher and higher rate standards are available and being used in high-performance backbone applications. As of this writing in 2020, Ethernet standards at 25, 40, 50, 100, 200 and

400 Gbit/s are all available, but each has specific requirements and design impacts. At these incredibly high speeds, interconnections and connection media become critical, and the copper and fiber cable requirements are in constant evolution, so you'll need to do some research to find out what to use (and why!) if you have applications running at these incredible bandwidths.

> Ethernet technology has advanced tremendously since its introduction, and several versions, in fact, are now obsolete, but I'll mention them here just for historical background. 10BASE5, or "ThickNet," was the original Ethernet, and was often called "Frozen Yellow Garden Hose" because the 13 mm diameter coaxial cable was huge, hard to work with, and yellow. 10BASE2, or "ThinNet," was a second-generation Ethernet. It used 5 mm diameter coax and BNC connectors in a bus topology to send 10 Mbit/s over network distances of 200 meters. Each node was connected using a "T" BNC connector, and the ends of a line had to be electrically terminated. With the robust BNC connector, 10BASE2 was originally adopted by entertainment manufacturers, and it's the first network I worked with for lighting control in the mid 1990s. 10BASE-T sent 10Mbit/s over Cat 5 and was one of the first Ethernet types to become widely used in our industry, although it was superseded by 100BASE-T and then 1000BASE-T.

ETHERNET HARDWARE

You can't have an Ethernet network without hardware components; let's work through an overview:

Network Interface Controller

The **Network Interface Controller** (NIC) is the actual interface between a computer and a physical network. From a hardware perspective, you might consider the NIC to actually be the network "node," although functionally, the whole device encompassing the NIC could of course also be thought of as the node. Historically, the NIC was a peripheral card (and was called Network Interface Card) but the NIC is now likely to be integrated directly into a device.

For a LAN of only two nodes, it is possible to connect the two devices by simply using a Cat 5e cable, but the transmit and receive lines need to be switched appropriately. To accomplish this in the old days, you would use a crossover or "direct connection" cable. However, most Ethernet interfaces built from the late

2000s onward do automatic transmit/receive configuration using **Auto-MDIX** (MDI stands for automatic Medium Dependent Interconnection; the X stands for "crossover").

> In the mid 1990s, when Ethernet started gaining acceptance in our industry, switches existed, but hubs—or "concentrators"—were the only network devices that were affordable (with affordable meaning about $1,500 for a four-port hub, hardly worth $1.50 today). To expand the LAN, we would just connect a second hub to the first, and so on, until we hit some limitations. The limits included the "5-4-3" rule, which managed collision domains and network diameters, and said you could have a maximum of five segments tied together with up to four repeaters, with no more than three segments containing active senders. This scheme was effective, but wasted bandwidth and had problems with data collisions that degraded network performance. Fortunately full-duplex switches became cost effective in the 2000s.

Hubs

Now mostly obsolete, hubs were the central connection point for a "hub and spoke" (star) topology LAN. The "repeating" hub had a number of hardware interfaces, receiving networking messages from any interface, connecting the transmit and receive lines correctly, and then repeating those messages to *every other connected device*.

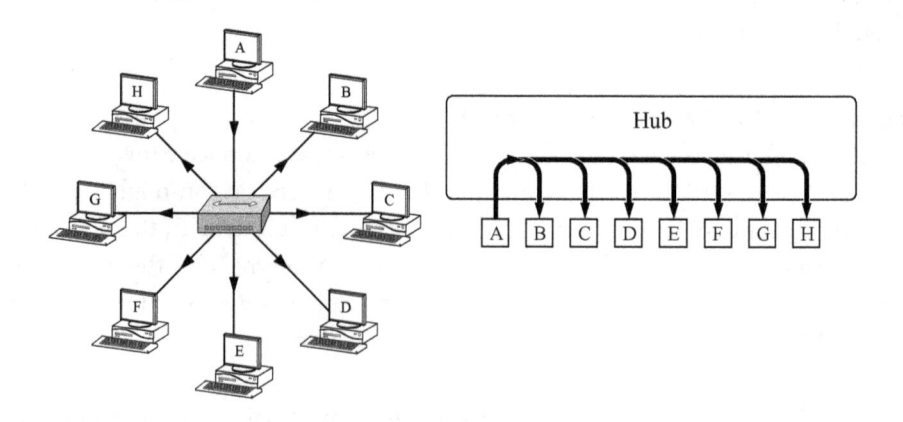

Repeating hubs operate at OSI layer 1, and do not contain any intelligence about the traffic they are carrying, which makes them very inefficient since all data has to broadcast to every port, regardless of whether or not the port needs the information. For this and other reasons, for just about every application today you should use a switch.

Switches

Switches (previously called "switching hubs") are the primary connection device for show networks, and contain enough internal intelligence to know the OSI layer 2 MAC address of each connected device and into which physical interface it is connected. By keeping track of which MAC addresses are associated with each interface, the switch can forward only the messages intended for a particular node, creating virtual "private channels."

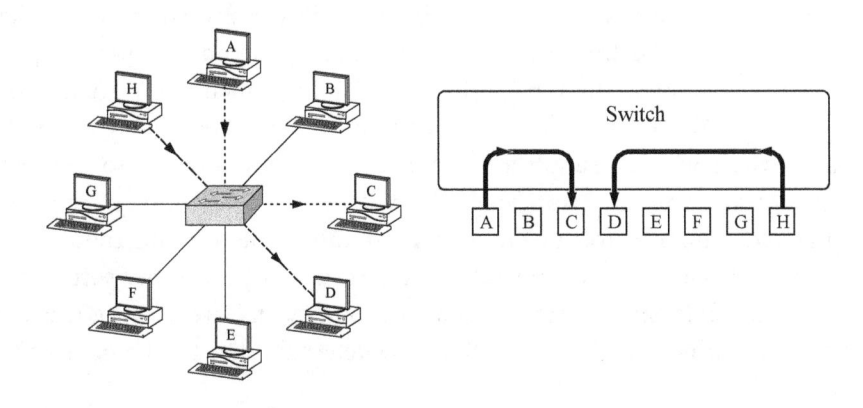

Hubs were very simple; they simply just broadcast every received frame. A switch, on the other hand, has three options for any incoming frame: it can **forward** the frame on to another interface based on the frame's Layer 2 destination address; it can **filter** the frame if it doesn't belong on a particular interface (or if there's some critical error); or, for frames sent to addresses the switch doesn't know, or frames sent to the broadcast address, the switch can send a copy of the frame out to all interfaces *except* the one on which the frame arrived. This process is called **flooding**. Why does the switch not send the frame back to the interface that delivered it? This approach prevents frames from bouncing back and forth if two switches are connected.

While early switches used CSMA/CD, **full-duplex switches** take the switching concept one step further, providing circuitry to enable each node to transmit and receive simultaneously on separate pairs of wires. With this approach, collision detection and avoidance mechanisms can actually be disabled, since with only two connected nodes and full-duplex communication, there *can't be any collisions*.

The "switching fabric" of the highest-performance switches, sometimes called **line-rate** switches, can operate at full "wire speed" for all the connected ports' possible total bandwidth. These can cost a bit more but are usually worth it for show networking applications.

In a network with an all full-duplex switching infrastructure, effective point-to-point communications to and from all network nodes simultaneously can be achieved, since each node sees only the traffic destined for it—many virtual communications channels can be active simultaneously. Full-duplex switches are used in most show networking applications.

Managed and Multi-Layer Switches

Many simple show networks can be built from simple, **unmanaged switches**, which come configured from the factory for basic operation. For more sophisticated network configuration and operation, like implementing Virtual LANs (VLANs, page 67), or enabling and disabling network features, you need a **managed switch**, which is simply a switch that can be configured in some way by a user or network administrator. Managed switches for entertainment can often be configured using controls on the unit itself; others allow configuration via a Web-based interface, via a command line interface (CLI), or other software. A **multilayer switch** is one that offers some functionality on Layer 3 or higher (typically simple routing, etc.); most multilayer switches also need to be managed in some way.

Energy-Efficient Ethernet (EEE)

As big as the entertainment industry is, the number of network nodes on every show in the world combined is still a small fraction of the larger networking world of offices and homes. For this reason, features are implemented that make sense on a larger system but cause us problems; Energy-Efficient Ethernet (EEE) is one of those. EEE is designed and implemented into switches so that in a large office building on a weekend when no one is working, electrical power on the network can be reduced, saving electricity. While laudable in terms of saving electricity, in show networks, however, this feature can cause control or media streaming devices that aren't in regular communication to become inaccessible on the network. And so EEE is a feature that you may need to turn off to keep things working properly; keep in mind too that some inexpensive switches have EEE permanently implemented and it can not be disabled.

Routers

While switches and hubs are used to create LANs, **routers** are used to connect LANs together.

For example, lighting and video could be using separate networks, but for some applications the two need to communicate; the router would be used to connect them together. Additionally, routers are used to connect LANs to the Internet. Routers operate in OSI Layer 3 (network) and are covered further on page 72.[2]

Media Converters and Bridges

A media converter is typically a two-port device, with one type of media on one port and another type on the other and operating on Layer 1.

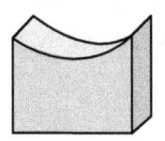

For instance, a media converter might convert UTP cable on one port to fiber on the other. Sometimes, network segments need to be connected together on Layer 2 without a router, and hardware to do this is called a **bridge**. This is commonly done when connecting between wired and wireless network segments.

POWER OVER ETHERNET (POE)

Since so many devices these days have an RJ-45 (8P8C) Ethernet connection, the IT industry decided that it would be great to deliver power along with the data connection, so in 2003 they developed IEEE 802.3af **Power over Ethernet** (PoE). The original scheme can deliver up to about 13 watts of DC power at 48V by sending power in a similar way to the way 48 VDC phantom power is delivered to a microphone; the 2009 version (802.3at) can deliver about 25 watts using all four pairs of cable, and 2018's 802.3bt, can deliver up to 90 watts. In the larger IT industry, probably the widest use of this technology is for Voice Over IP (VOIP) phones; a single cable run from a PoE switch can provide power and a data connection. On shows, we might see PoE used for Wireless Access Points (page 30), cameras, control protocol gateway, and various kinds of low-power devices.

---

2 Note: In home networking, the device called a "router" typically does far more, and incorporates a switch, probably a "wireless access point (see the "IEEE 802.11 "Wi-Fi"" section on page 164) and the ability to assign network addresses automatically using DHCP (page 39)..

In the PoE scheme, Power Sourcing Equipment (PSE) provides 48 VDC (same as audio phantom power) over the Cat 5e cable, and is used by the Powered Device (PD). As in audio phantom power, since DC power is used, it doesn't interfere with the Ethernet data signal, but the amount of power that can be delivered is limited by the current carrying capacity of the Cat 5e cable. There are two types of devices that provide PoE. A device that can provide it at the end of a run, like an Ethernet switch, is called an "endspan" device. A device that sits inline and provides PoE (often called a PoE injector), is referred to as a "midspan" device. To ensure that non-PoE equipment is not damaged if connected, a procedure is implemented at startup to ensure that power will only be delivered to connected devices configured to accept it.

PoE, like many networking technologies, is under constant development and there are many new varieties in development at any time; check with your manufacturer and be sure to research the current state of the technology before buying anything.

IEEE 802.11 "WI-FI"

The IEEE **802.11** "wireless Ethernet" standard revolutionized the portable computer market, and found many applications in our market as well, especially during the programming or tech of a show. IEEE 802.11, which is also called "Wi-Fi®" (after the Wi-Fi Alliance trade association for 802.11 manufacturers), offers high-speed, easy-to-use connections to mobile computer users. Of course, that also means it can provide convenient access to us for show networking, as long as we use the systems carefully and prudently. Wi-Fi is based on "spread spectrum"[3] radio transmission, where the transmitted frequency jumps around in coordination with the receiver. This makes it a very powerful transmission medium that accommodates interference pretty well.

The basic operational concepts of 802.11 for typical applications are simple. Typically, a **Wireless Access Point** (WAP) is connected (through a standard Cat 5e cable) to a network, and through that network to the Internet. The WAP then acts as a "bridge" to the network, allowing portable devices to connect to it using data transmission over radio frequency (RF) electromagnetic radiation. The various 802.11 standards operate in bands allocated by the FCC for industrial, scientific, and medical (ISM) use.

Wi-Fi, like many networking technologies, is under constant development and

---

3 Patented in 1942 by the actress Hedy Lamarr and the composer George Antheil (best known for his *Ballet Mécanique*, which involved many forms of synchronization).

there are many new varieties in development at any time; check with your manufacturer and be sure to research the current state of the technology before buying anything. But as of 2020, 802.11 network types include the following (from earliest to latest):

IEEE Type	Max Rate	Frequency Band
802.11a	54 Mbit/s	5 GHz
802.11b	11 Mbit/s	2.4 GHz
802.11g	54 Mbit/s	2.4 GHz
802.11n	600 Mbit/s	2.4, 5 GHz
802.11ac	6,933 Mbit/s	5 GHz
802.11ax	9,608 Mbit/s	1-6, 2.4, 5 GHz

Basic Structure

There are four basic components of an 802.11 network: stations, access points (AP or WAP), the wireless medium, and the distribution system. Stations are simply the computers you want to connect to the network. Access points are the "bridge" between the wireless and wired networks (or, in some cases, between wireless devices). APs also provide the critical functionality of converting wired MAC frames to wireless, and vice-versa, and manage radio transmission. The radio signals are, of course, the physical medium (radio waves rather than electrons on a cable) that is used to transport the data. Finally, the distribution system, which is somewhat confusingly labeled, is the logical process by which potentially-moving, connected stations are allowed to move through and between various parts of the wireless network.

Service Set IDentifier

Each wireless network is given a **Service Set IDentifier** (SSID), which identifies that network through an ASCII string up to 32 characters long. This is the "network name" that users see when they turn their laptops on and select a wireless network.

Security Issues

Wired networks have some built-in security, in that you can exert some control over who plugs into your network. However, as soon as you connect an open, unsecured access point to your wired network, you are opening up your network—and therefore everything connected to it—to anyone within radio range since, by definition, wireless frames are broadcast to everyone in range.

Some users will disable SSID beacons and configure their WAPs; this does offer a bit of security, in that casual users cannot see or access the network. However, anyone monitoring the channel (albeit with more technical skill than the average user) will be able to see the SSID in the request/response interchange. Hiding the SSID can also cause problems with some equipment. A more restrictive practice would be to use MAC ID filtering, allowing only specific hardware interfaces to connect to a network[4].

So for all applications, WiFi security is very important, although it's too much of a moving target to document in a fixed medium like a book. Enabling security is usually a simple matter of configuring the WAP using its setup procedure, and of course any security—even if flawed (like some of the early wireless security schemes)—is better than none at all.

Should You Use Wi-Fi On Your Show?

My advice for all show applications: *If you can use a wire (or fiber), use a wire!* 802.11 offers fantastic utility that is especially useful for the (noncritical) programming phase of any project; being able to walk around a venue with a wireless laptop or handheld device offers amazing flexibility and ease of use. However, this utility comes with some security risks, as detailed above, and tremendous potential reliability issues, since it operates in unlicensed bands, meaning that you have absolutely no way to know (or regulate) who else is operating in that band. You may be able to keep them out of your system using security procedures, but you can't keep them from (maybe even unintentionally) interfering with your system, which can cause delays or even failures in data transmission. In addition, radio is, by definition, a "shared" media, meaning that it has none of the advantages of a switched, full-duplex structure that is so important to our market.

If you only need Wi-Fi for the programming period of the show, that's great and then just disable it once you're done. If there is no possible way to use a hardwire connection, then use wireless, but be sure to carefully research and implement your system, and also include in your design a way to monitor transmission and interference issues. Again, if you can use a wire (or fiber, of course), use a wire! More on this in "Show Networking Best Practices" on page 77.

---

4   MAC addresses can be "spoofed" by advanced users.

WHY ETHERNET IS GOOD FOR OUR INDUSTRY

Ethernet rightfully got off to a slow start in our industry. The nondeterministic nature of CSMA/CD, with its random back-off collision recovery time, was on its own enough to scare off many entertainment engineers in the early days. However, over the years, the IT industry has (fortuitously for us) solved this and many of our other objections, and full-duplex, switched Ethernet is an excellent digital highway solution for shows. To summarize, it offers us the following:

- Open standard
- High bandwidth
- Low cost
- Low-latency delivery using full-duplex switches
- Electrical isolation
- High-quality CRC error check of every single frame transmitted across the network
- "Guaranteed" delivery through the use of TCP or other related protocols

These reasons and others are why Ethernet came to become the dominant network for shows. With that in place, let's move on to issues of network systems.

Chapter 3

NETWORK OPERATIONS

Now that we have introduced basic networking concepts and hardware, let's move into some of the underlying components and processes that make networks work. Unfortunately for those of us (like me) who are very hands-on people, these concepts are very abstract. But hang in there; we only need the basics, and these concepts are important to learn.

The **Transmission Control Protocol** (TCP), **User Datagram Protocol** (UDP), and **Internet Protocol** (IP) are the backbone of networks, including, of course, the network of networks: the Internet. TCP, UDP, and IP are separate protocols, but are often used together in a protocol "suite" or "stack". These protocols were developed in the late 1970s, before the OSI layer standard was finalized, but TCP and UDP can be thought of as occupying OSI Layer 4 (transport), with IP fitting into OSI layer 3 (network). This means that TCP/IP or UDP/IP sit *above* networks like Ethernet, which occupies OSI Layers 2 and 1, and *below* user processes or programs such as a web browser, which uses HyperText Transfer Protocol (HTTP). Here is a simplified table showing how the various protocols align with OSI, and the units they transmit:

Layer	Name	Function	Unit
7	Application	DNS, FTP, HTTP, IMAP, IRC, NNTP, POP3, SIP, SMTP, etc.	Data
6	Presentation	data compression, data encryption, etc.	
5	Session	full-duplex, half-duplex, etc.	
4	Transport	TCP, UDP, etc.	Segments
3	Network	IP	Packets/ Datagrams
2	Data link	Ethernet MAC and LLC layers	Frames
1	Physical	Ethernet PHY layer	Bits

While those in entertainment may have encountered these network protocols in conjunction with Ethernet, they were actually designed to handle traffic across a variety of networks, platforms, and systems, and accomplish this, for the most part, transparently to the user. Their work is so transparent, in fact, that many of the operational details of these protocols are beyond the scope of this book; however, the general characteristics of the protocols are important to understand.

TRANSMISSION CONTROL PROTOCOL (TCP)

IP makes no guarantee to services residing on higher layers that a packet will get to a particular destination; it simply makes its "best effort." TCP, on the other hand, is a **connection-oriented**, **reliable** protocol, meaning that it can guarantee that packets will arrive intact and can be reassembled in the right order. TCP provides this reliability by creating a "virtual circuit" connection to the receiver, which must be specifically established and terminated. Using the connection (and other features of the protocol), TCP guarantees to the layers above it that a message will make it to its destination somehow, or else it will notify the upper layers that the transmission failed. TCP is used in many show networking applications where the integrity of the transmitted data is of paramount importance, such as a motion control or pyro command.

USER DATAGRAM PROTOCOL (UDP)

UDP takes an **unreliable** approach to **connectionlessly** deliver **datagrams**. Without TCP's overhead packaging packets for delivery and dealing with the connection, UDP can be much faster and more efficient. Of course, "unreliable" UDP may, on the right network, be quite reliable, and UDP is used in many entertainment applications where speed of delivery is of the essence and the network is stable and not heavily loaded, which ensures for the most part that the packets will be sent across intact and in order. Alternatively, UDP can be used with other protocols handling the reliable transmission aspects of the communication process.

INTERNET PROTOCOL (IP)

To be delivered properly to its destination, a postal letter needs an address unique to that destination. Similarly, each packet of data on a network needs a destination address, and handling this information is one of the key functions of the **Internet Protocol** (IP). IP version 4 (IPv4) is the backbone of the vast majority of show networks,[1] and it provides a universal addressing scheme that can work within or between a wide variety of networks (hence the "inter" name), providing unique IDs for the connected hosts. An "IP address" is simply a 32-bit binary number

---

1 IPv6 (page 53) is also used and is gaining some acceptance in the 2020s, but IPv4 will likely be used for many years to come so we're starting with it here.

uniquely assigned to a machine on a particular network, and 32 bits gives us 4,294,967,296 unique addresses. 32-bit binary numbers are pretty unwieldy for humans to deal with, so we usually deal with IP addresses using **dot-decimal notation**, with each three-digit decimal number representing one eight-bit **octet** of the full address (an octet is an 8-bit chunk of a binary number; this term replaced the more ambiguous "byte"—see "Appendix: Numbering Systems" on page 115 for more information). In dot-decimal format, the IP address range goes from `0.0.0.0` to `255.255.255.255`. So, while we might refer to a dotted-decimal address like `192.168.13.66`, what the network is transmitting—and the connected network devices are dealing with—is of course binary, in this case: `11000000 10101000 00001101 01000010`. IPv4 addresses traditionally break down into two parts: a **Network IDentifier** for a particular network (remember that IP was designed to connect networks together), and a **Host IDentifier** unique for a particular device (lighting console, video server, projector, moving light, I/O device, etc.) on that network.

Address Classes

IPv4 addresses were also originally divided into five classes, with varying numbers of bits assigned to the Network ID and the Host ID. Even though the classes have been replaced for their original purposes, the terminology still used, so let's cover a brief overview. Class A networks assign 7 bits to the Network ID and 24 bits to the host; this type of address was intended for very large organizations with many hosts. Class B networks assign 14 bits to the Network ID and 16 bits to the host for intermediate size networks, while Class C assigned 21 bits to the Network ID, and only 8 bits to hosts, which allowed many small organizations, each with a few hundred hosts at a maximum (like most show networks), so Class C addresses are very commonly used in our field:

Class	*IP Address*	*Networks*	*Hosts*
A	0nnnnnnn hhhhhhhh hhhhhhhh hhhhhhhh 7-bit Network ID, 24-bit Host ID	128	16,777,216
B	10nnnnnn nnnnnnnn hhhhhhhh hhhhhhhh 14-bit Network ID, 16-bit Host ID	16,384	65,536
C	110nnnnn nnnnnnnn nnnnnnnn hhhhhhhh 21-bit Network ID, 8-bit Host ID	2,097,152	256
D	1110mmmm mmmmmmmm mmmmmmmm mmmmmmmm 28-bit multicast address		
E	1111rrrr rrrrrrrr rrrrrrrr rrrrrrrr Reserved for future use		

In the early days of IP, this scheme worked well, and would easily allow every computer on the planet to be connected. However, as the Internet grew, this scheme proved to be inefficient, since addresses were often assigned in blocks that might not match the needs of an organization—a small company with only 100 hosts could be allocated an address range that blocked out tens of thousands of IP addresses. To get around this problem (and others), things like Classless Inter-Domain Routing (CIDR) and Network Address Translation (NAT, page 75) were developed.

Multicast Addresses

Class D addresses are reserved for a special purpose: multicasting, where one device may need to send packets to multiple receivers simultaneously. Multicasting might be used for streaming audio or video media where there may be many receivers of the transmission, or by a lighting console that needs to send its data to a number of processing units that do something with that data. The range of IP addresses assigned for this purpose is `224.0.0.0` through `239.255.255.255`; receivers can join the multicast group using Internet Group Management Protocol (IGMP, page 75).

Broadcast Address

One specially reserved address is `255.255.255.255`, which is the **broadcast IP address**. This is used when a packet must reach all connected nodes (more on page 63). Because all nodes have to process the traffic, it is inefficient both for the network and loading of connected devices. For this reason, broadcast transmission is used sparingly.

Loopback/Localhost IP Address

Another reserved address is the **loopback** address, which is typically `127.0.0.1`.[2] The loopback address allows a packet to be sent from the **local host** back to itself. This can be used for testing, or when an IP process needs to communicate with another IP process on the same machine.

Private IP Addresses

For shows, we very often build closed (non-Internet connected) networks and, therefore, could probably just use whatever IP address we felt like. However, this is not a good practice, because if any of those machines using an allocated public IP address were to be accidentally connected to the Internet, conflicts could occur, causing problems.

---

[2] In IPv6, the loopback address is ::1

Instead, it's good practice for show networks to use addresses set aside within each class for **private networking**; these addresses are also called **nonroutable**, since they do not belong on the public Internet and are generally blocked by routers.

Class	Start of Range	End of Range
A	10.0.0.0	10.255.255.255
B	172.16.0.0	172.31.255.255
C	192.168.0.0	192.168.255.255

Note that not all of these addresses are available for allocation to hosts. Addresses like 192.168.x.0 are reserved for the "network address" or "network ID"; addresses like 192.168.x.255 or 255.255.255.255 are reserved for "broadcast" address usage.

SETTING IP ADDRESSES

While there are many aspects to the Internet Protocol, the primary concept that show techs need to be comfortable with is the IP Address. There are many ways that IP Addresses can be assigned to nodes on a network, but in the end each connected device on a network needs a unique IP address. Let's take a look at three ways IP addresses are managed in show networks.

Dynamic Host Configuration Protocol (DHCP)

In the vast majority of commercial and consumer networks, the IP address of each of the connected hosts is automatically assigned using the **Dynamic Host Configuration Protocol** (DHCP), which allows a node to obtain an IP address "lease" automatically. When a device is shut off, disconnected from a network, or the lease expires, that IP address can be released for use by others. The DHCP process starts when the IP protocols are initiated on a machine connected to the network; usually this occurs right after power up. The device requesting an IP address sends a UDP packet to 255.255.255.255, the broadcast IP address that all nodes on that subnet will receive. If a **DHCP server** (which could be a stand alone device or a software process built into another device) is available on that network, it replies with an offer of an IP address (and some other information like the Default Gateway, more on page 72). If the host accepts the offer, the IP address is "leased" for a period of time. Here are four exchanges captured from an actual DHCP negotiation using the WireShark® packet capture and analysis software:

Time	Source	Destination	Protocol	Info
26.323156	0.0.0.0	255.255.255.255	DHCP	DHCP Discover
26.325810	192.168.1.1	192.168.1.180	DHCP	DHCP Offer
26.329842	0.0.0.0	255.255.255.255	DHCP	DHCP Request
26.333972	192.168.1.1	192.168.1.180	DHCP	DHCP ACK

The first line shows a host sending out a "DHCP Discover" message, looking for a DHCP server on the network; this is sent to the broadcast address of 255.255.255.255. In this case, there is a DHCP server available at 192.168.1.1, and it responds with an offer of the IP address 192.168.1.180 (some details omitted for clarity), and the host accepts it. The whole process takes about 20 milliseconds. Finally, one important note to keep in mind: there should be only one DHCP server available on a given network; multiple servers can cause very difficult-to-troubleshoot havoc.

DHCP Reservation

DHCP servers know the Layer 2 MAC address of connected devices through the process outlined above. Most DHCP servers have the ability to consistently assign the same IP address to a particular device based on its MAC address, and this is sometimes used as the basis of a network management technique called "DHCP Reservation." With this approach, the DHCP server is used to maintain a master IP assignment list, and all the other devices on the network are set to automatically get their addresses via DHCP. In a complex network with many kinds of devices, each of which might get its IP address set in a different way, this technique can offer centralized management and configuration; if a device is changed, the network administrator just has to update the table in the DHCP server with the new MAC address. This approach does have some security vulnerabilities, in that a rogue DHCP server on the network could take over, but this can be dealt with in other ways.

Link-Local Addresses

If a DHCP server is not available, a host can determine its own unique **link-local** address, intended only for use within the local network segment (packets containing these addresses are not forwarded by routers). IPv4 addresses 169.254.1.0 through 169.254.254.255 are assigned for this purpose. These addresses can be manually assigned, but more typically the host's operating system sets them automatically using "stateless address autoconfiguration," which selects an address using a random procedure, and then checks on the network using ARP (page 50) to make sure the address is not already in use. The function that handles link-local address assignment is sometimes called Automatic Private IP Addressing (APIPA) or auto-IP.

Static/Fixed IP Addresses

Rather than being configured automatically by DHCP, as is common with most home and office networks, devices with "static" or "fixed" IP addresses need to be configured manually by the network administrator. Fixed-IP addressing schemes can be used for important devices on a network that don't change (like a server or a printer in an office network), for devices which communicate using simple protocols that aren't capable of discovering connected devices, or for networks where the network administrator wants to lock down and control all the connected devices.

USEFUL COMMANDS WORKING WITH IP ADDRESSES

While there are many commands and utilities for working with networks, there are two widely used commands that exist in most operating systems and embedded in many devices that are very useful and worth mentioning here.

ipconfig/ifconfig Command

It's easy to see what IP information has been assigned to your system; from Windows®, you can use a command-line utility called `ipconfig`; on a macOS® it's `ifconfig` from the terminal.

Typing `ipconfig` from the Windows Command Prompt, for example, you would get something like this, enabling you to verify (or discover) the configured address (excerpt only shown for clarity):

```
C:\>ipconfig

Ethernet adapter Local Area Connection:

   Connection-specific DNS Suffix  . :
   IPv4 Address. . . . . . . . . . . : 192.168.1.101
   Subnet Mask . . . . . . . . . . . : 255.255.255.0
   Default Gateway . . . . . . . . . : 192.168.1.1
```

Note that there is a lot more on the subnet mask starting on page 43; the default gateway is covered on page 72.

From the `ipconfig` command line, you can also configure and view a number of other parameters about your IP connection. Typing `ipconfig ?` will give you a complete list of options.

Ping

Once you have all your network devices connected and configured, an easy way to verify that they are working properly on the network is to **ping** them. `ping` sends some special packets, called Internet Control Message Protocol (ICMP) echo requests, to the device at the IP address[3] that you want to test. It then tracks responses from that machine and gives you some timing information.

For example, let's ping the machine at `192.168.1.21`:

```
C:\>ping 192.168.1.21

Pinging 192.168.1.21 with 32 bytes of data:
Reply from 192.168.1.21: bytes=32 time<1ms TTL=64
Reply from 192.168.1.21: bytes=32 time<1ms TTL=64
Reply from 192.168.1.21: bytes=32 time<1ms TTL=64
Reply from 192.168.1.21: bytes=32 time<1ms TTL=64

Ping statistics for 192.168.1.21:
    Packets: Sent = 4, Received = 4, Lost = 0 0% loss),
Approximate round trip times in milli-seconds:
    Minimum = 0ms, Maximum = 0ms, Average = 0ms
```

"`<1ms`" is the time measured for the destination machine to respond and for the packets to transfer down the network. 1 ms is pretty fast, but this is not unusual for a closed, small network. If an IP address (or other configuration information) is not valid, or a machine on the network is not responding properly, you can see an error like this:

```
C:\>ping 10.0.0.26

Pinging 10.0.0.26 with 32 bytes of data:

Request timed out.
Request timed out.
Request timed out.
Request timed out.

Ping statistics for 10.0.0.26:
    Packets: Sent = 4, Received = 0, Lost = 4 100% loss),
```

There are many options for the ping command—type `ping` with no arguments to see a complete list. But the basic ping command tells you a lot: the connected machines are powered up and connected to the network, the cable is at least min-

---

3   It's also possible to ping a domain, such as www.controlgeek.net, instead of a numeric IP address; although for this to work you also need a Domain Name System (page 75)—and a gateway to the Internet (page 72).

imally functioning, and—importantly—the two devices are in the same subnet:

SUBNETS

A key advantage of networks is that they can scale; with larger networks comes complexity, and for security and operational reasons it often makes sense to break networks into smaller **subnets**. Because we use general-purpose computing equipment designed to work on any size network, we have to deal with concepts such as subnet masks even when we are connecting only a handful of machines in a private, closed network. As a result, we need to wade into this topic, which is probably the most challenging networking topic to many show techs. Also, we will be talking a bit of binary here; if you need a review see "Appendix: Numbering Systems" on page 115.

As we discussed, IP addresses are broken down into network bits and host bits; in addition, network address space can be divided further into subnets. But for the sysetm to understand what is going on we need to indicate to the system somehow where we are positioning the boundary between the network bits and the host bits; setting this boundary is the simple (and widely misunderstood) purpose of the **subnet mask**.

The computer, of course, deals with the subnet mask (and everything else) in binary, and, at a very low level, nodes on the network can rapidly check to see if a particular address is part of its subnet by comparing (using a "bitwise AND" logical operation) each bit of the addresses with the subnet mask. Because the mask is defining the boundary between the network bits and the host bits and there can be only one boundary, the mask must start with a contiguous block of 1 bits and finish with a contiguous block of 0 bits. This is likely getting very confusing, so here is an example of the subnet mask `255.255.255.0` applied to the IP address `192.168.1.107`:

```
192       168       1         107       IP address
255       255       255       0         Subnet mask
11000000  10101000  00000001  01101011  IP address in binary
11111111  11111111  11111111  00000000  Subnet mask in binary
11000000  10101000  00000001  00000000  Network ID
```

With 8 bits of the host portion of the address available, using this subnet mask we can address up to 254 hosts using the address range `192.168.1.1` to `192.168.1.254` (`192.168.1.0` is reserved for the subnet identifier; `192.168.1.255` is the broadcast address for this subnet).

The contiguous block of 1 bits makes for some seemingly strange dotted-decimal subnet masks; and another way of indicating the subnet mask is to append a "/" and the number of subnet mask bits to the IP address. For example, the IP address shown above, when used with the `255.255.255.0` subnet, could also be shown as `192.168.1.107/24`. You may see both forms of nomenclature.

Let's look at another example, with the subnet mask `255.255.240.0 (/20)` and the IP address `10.43.26.222`:

```
10         43         26         222       IP address
255        255        240        0         Subnet mask
00001010   00101110   00011010   11011110  IP address in binary
11111111   11111111   11110000   00000000  Subnet mask in binary
00001010   00101110   00010000   00000000  Network ID
```

This subnet mask leaves 12 possible bits for host IDs and the host range for this subnet would be `10.43.16.1` to `10.43.31.254`. I didn't calculate this in my head; I simply went online and used a free subnet calculator.[4]

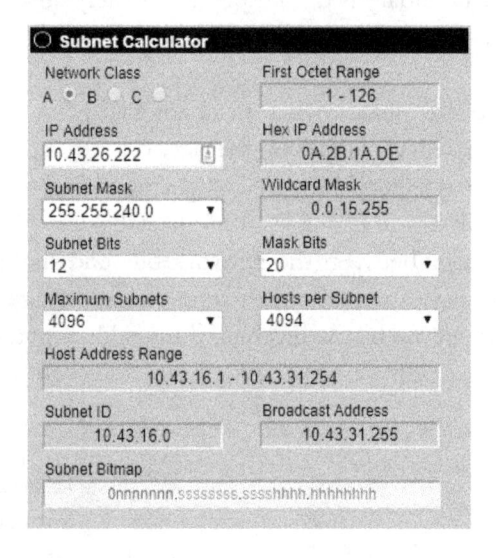

Subnet Calculator	
Network Class	First Octet Range
A ● B ○ C ○	1 - 126
IP Address	Hex IP Address
10.43.26.222	0A.2B.1A.DE
Subnet Mask	Wildcard Mask
255.255.240.0	0.0.15.255
Subnet Bits	Mask Bits
12	20
Maximum Subnets	Hosts per Subnet
4096	4094
Host Address Range	
10.43.16.1 - 10.43.31.254	
Subnet ID	Broadcast Address
10.43.16.0	10.43.31.255
Subnet Bitmap	
0nnnnnnn.sssssss.sssshhhh.hhhhhhhh	

A Simplified Subnet Mask Approach

In large networks at giant corporations, there are times where the network designers have to squeeze out every possible available IP address; efficient subnetting is an important thing in these situations. However, many show networks are simple

---

4 `http://www.subnet-calculator.com/`

44 • **CHAPTER 3: NETWORK OPERATIONS**

enough that we can use a much simpler, less efficient method: setting the subnet by whole octet.

So with this approach, we only use three possible subnet masks:

Simplified Approach Subnet Masks
255.000.000.000
255.255.000.000
255.255.255.000

Here, we are looking for whole octets of the IP address to match, and we don't have to worry about all the binary details.

Here's a table showing several IP addresses with the same subnet mask, illustrating which will work and which won't.

IP Address	
192.168.201.001	Main IP
255.255.255.000	Subnet Mask for all hosts
192.168.202.123	Can it communicate? No
192.168.201.234	Can it communicate? Yes
192.168.001.234	Can it communicate? No
192.168.201.101	Can it communicate? Yes

With this approach, we certainly waste some possible host addresses, but until we start commonly building networks with thousands of connected devices[5] we can afford to be a bit sloppier in order to make things easier to use and make this widely misunderstood topic easier to deal with.

Example Network with One Subnet

To bring all this together, let's look at an example. Let's say you have two devices on a network connected via a switch. One host is set to an IP address of 192.168.1.33; the other is set to 192.168.101.2. If you have the subnet mask set on both hosts to 255.255.255.0, these two devices will *not* be able to communicate because, with the subnet mask of 255.255.255.0, the first *three*

---

5 If you're building a network that big and complicated you probably want to go for IPv6 anyway.

octets of all the IP addresses on the subnet have to match exactly, and we have one device set to a subnet of `192.168.101`, while the other is set for `192.168.1`. So, the first three octets do *not* match, and these systems will not be able to communicate with each other on an IP network:

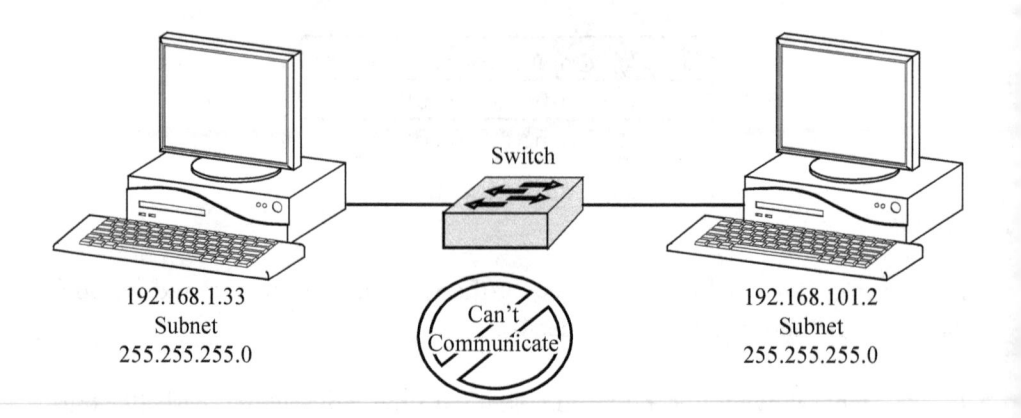

192.168.1.33
Subnet
255.255.255.0

Switch

Can't Communicate

192.168.101.2
Subnet
255.255.255.0

There are two easy solutions to this problem. First, you could change the subnet mask on both machines to `255.255.0.0`, meaning only the first two octets have to match:

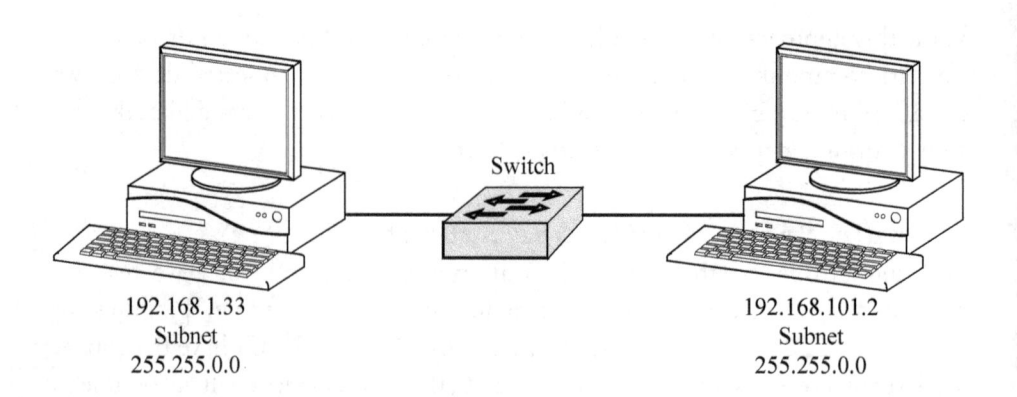

192.168.1.33
Subnet
255.255.0.0

Switch

192.168.101.2
Subnet
255.255.0.0

This approach means, though, that you effectively have one big `192.168.0.0` subnet, and you can't divide it further.

Alternatively, you could keep the original subnet mask of 255.255.255.0, and change one host's IP from 192.168.101.2 to 192.168.1.2:

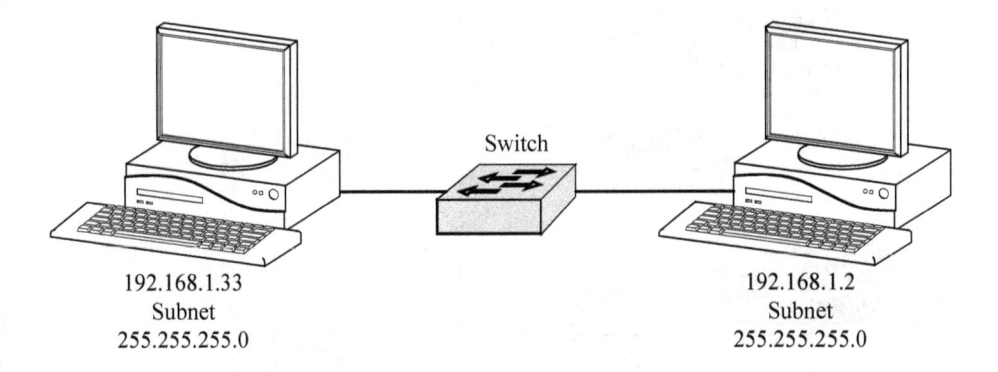

```
192.168.1.33                              192.168.1.2
Subnet                                    Subnet
255.255.255.0                             255.255.255.0
```

Alternatively, you could change the other host from 192.168.1.33 to 192.168.101.33:

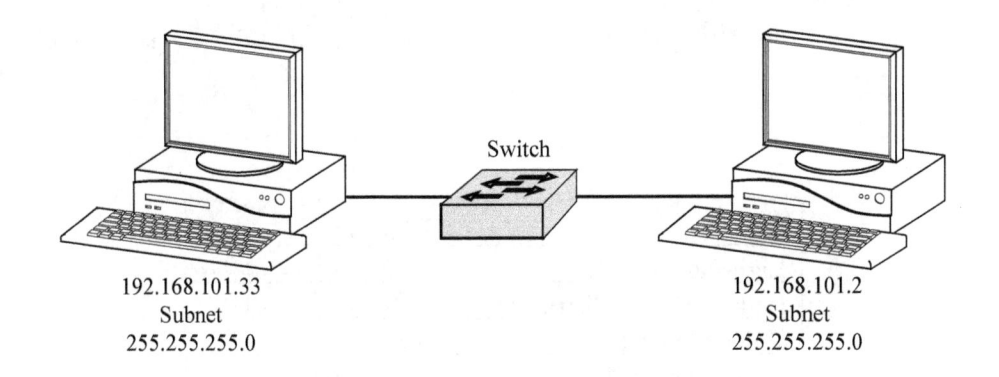

```
192.168.101.33                            192.168.101.2
Subnet                                    Subnet
255.255.255.0                             255.255.255.0
```

Example Network with Two Subnets
Let's look now at a slightly more complicated system, where lighting and video are sharing a single network[6].

---

6 Something I wouldn't generally advise, more on that on page 50

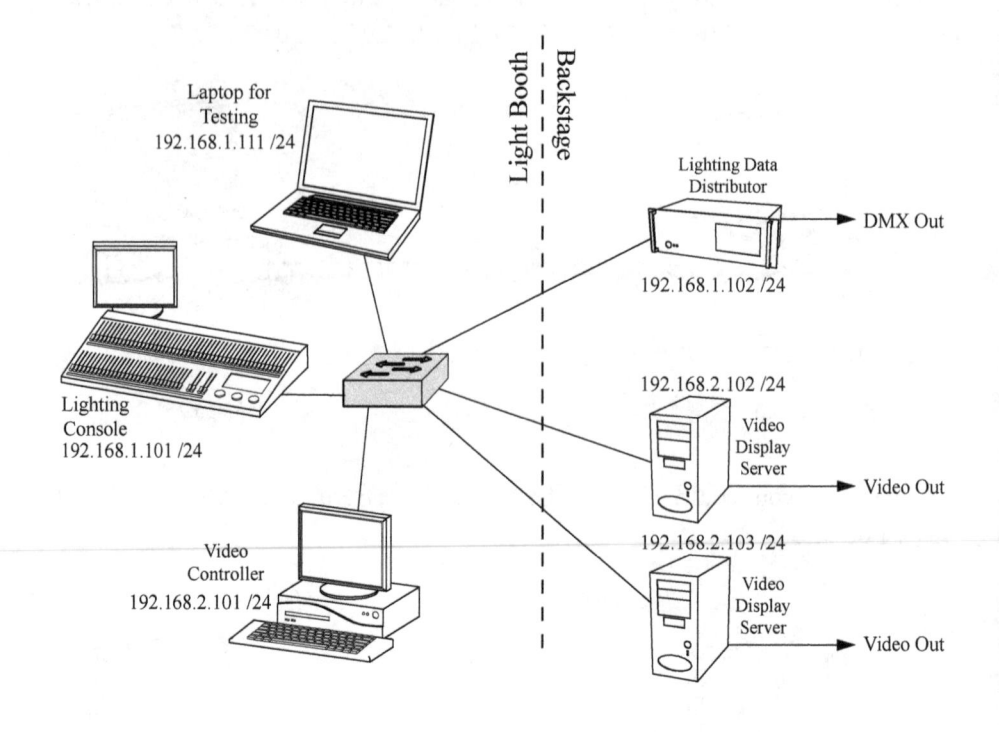

Host	IP Address
Lighting Console	192.168.1.101
Lighting Data Distributor	192.168.1.102
Video Controller	192.168.2.101
Video Display 1	192.168.2.102
Video Display 2	192.168.2.103
Laptop (Testing Only)	192.168.1.111

You'll notice in the table that the video system is on a different subnet than lighting: `192.168.2.x`. In this case, this was done because both our lighting and video systems use different methods for their own communications, and the systems are not inter-operable so there's no reason for these two systems to talk to each other. So to avoid any conflicts, and just to keep things organized, it's good practice to put them on two different subnets.

We've got everything configured and all the lighting devices respond just fine to a ping command, but then when we try to pin the video controller, we get this::

```
C:\>ping 192.168.2.101

Pinging 192.168.2.101 with 32 bytes of data:
Destination host unreachable.
Destination host unreachable.
Destination host unreachable.
Destination host unreachable.

Ping statistics for 192.168.2.101:
    Packets: Sent = 4, Received = 4, Lost = 0 0% loss)
```

Why is the destination host "unreachable"? It's plugged in and the Ethernet activity lights on all the connections are lit, so we know we have a physical connection. We try pinging the lighting console at `192.168.1.101`, and that works just fine. So that tells us our cable is good, the network is working, etc. So what's wrong?

It's one of the most common misunderstandings I see in network setup—our laptop is on the lighting `192.168.1.0` subnet, and we are trying to ping into the `192.168.2.0` subnet, with a subnet mask of `255.255.255.0`, which means that the first three octets of any host we are trying to reach must be exactly the same as the IP address of the machine from which you are sending the `ping` command.[7]

So for testing we change the address of the laptop to `192.168.2.111/24`—moving it onto the video subnet—and now we can ping from the laptop to the video machines just fine:

```
C:\>ping 192.168.2.101

Pinging 192.168.2.101 with 32 bytes of data:
Reply from 192.168.2.101: bytes=32 time=<1ms TTL=64
Reply from 192.168.2.101: bytes=32 time=<1ms TTL=64
Reply from 192.168.2.101: bytes=32 time=<1ms TTL=64
Reply from 192.168.2.101: bytes=32 time=<1ms TTL=64
```

---

[7] You could also do this with a router, see page 28

Physically Separated Topology

Let's address one final issue before moving on. The network as shown above—with two IP subnets on a single switch—can work just fine. However, both this lighting system and the video system output a lot of traffic and a simple, cheap switch might get overloaded handling all those packets and cause some delays or other glitches.

There's an easy solution to that—add another switch, and physically separate the networks:

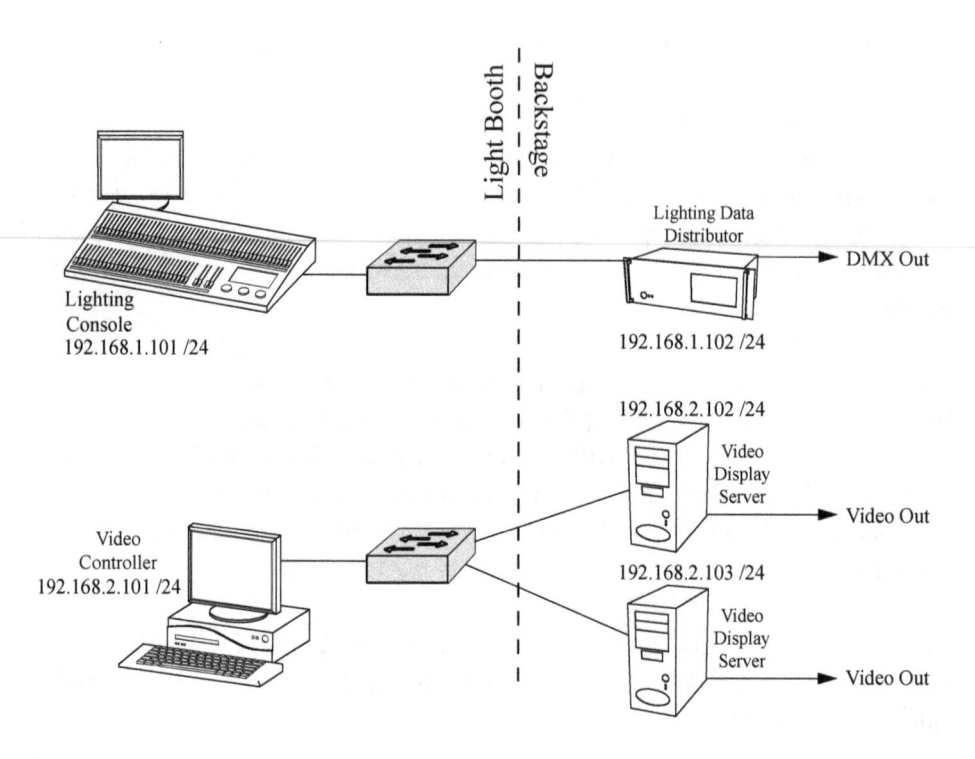

Even professional-grade show switches are relatively inexpensive in the big picture, and since there is no connection between the two systems, physically separating the systems offers many benefits: increased fault tolerance (one switch failure only takes down part of the show), isolation between systems, etc.

ADDRESS RESOLUTION PROTOCOL (ARP)

IP addresses were designed for inter-networking purposes and, as we have seen, IP addresses can be assigned to machines either manually by the system administrator or automatically by a process such as DHCP. Lower-level network communications, however, need to communicate down at a level closer to the hardware, and for this purpose machines have an additional unique physical "hardware address" such as the Ethernet MAC address. Resolving these physical addresses with IP addresses is the job of the **Address Resolution Protocol** (ARP), which maintains an ARP table, relating Layer 3 IP addresses to Layer 2 physical addresses.

To understand the basic ARP process, let's consider an example. A host on a private network needs to communicate with another host on the same private network. Unique layer 3 IP addresses have been configured into both machines, but the network system needs to find the layer 2 *physical* address of the second machine in order to put that low-level address into the frame used for communication. Because the sending system doesn't know this layer 2 physical address, the IP address is considered "unresolved," so the first machine sends an "ARP request" out onto the network. This ARP message is broadcast to all connected hosts, asking the owner of the target IP address to respond with its physical address.

Let's take a look at an actual message capture using Wireshark®. A user at a Dell® computer at 192.168.1.104 pings an macOS® host machine at 192.168.1.102. Because the network was just turned on, the system doesn't yet know the Ethernet MAC address of the Apple machine assigned the 192.168.1.102 IP address, so before it sends the ping messages, it sends an ARP request message out:

```
Source              Destination         Protocol  Length  Info
DellEsgP_88:e7:b6   Broadcast           ARP       106     who has 192.168.1.102? Tell 192.168.1.104
Apple_96:23:3a      DellEsgP_88:e7:b6   ARP       60      192.168.1.102 is at 00:23:32:96:23:3a
```

The first ARP request of "Who has 192.168.1.102?" is broadcast to the entire network segment because the sender has no idea of the Layer 2, Ethernet MAC address of the target. The Apple machine, which had been assigned the 102 address, now responds with, "192.168.1.102 is at 00:23:32:96:23:3a", which is the Apple's Ethernet MAC address in hex. Throughout this process, other hosts that see the ARP conversation can also note the same information "ARP cache" so they, too, will know the correlation between physical and IP addresses.

This ARP process takes less than a second, and the ping commands then go through.

ARP messages are also used when IP addresses are set to ensure that each host's IP address is unique on that network—having more than one host with the same IP address would cause all kinds of problems, and most operating systems will detect such conflicts and deliver to the user an error message. For example, let's say I set up a different machine and set it to the same, already-used address and connect it to the same network. Then the newly configured host will send a "Gratuitous ARP" for `192.168.1.102`:

```
Source             Destination        Protocol  Length  Info
DellEsgP_88:e7:b6  Broadcast          ARP       106     Gratuitous ARP for 192.168.1.102 (Request)
Apple_96:23:3a     DellEsgP_88:e7:b6  ARP       60      Gratuitous ARP for 192.168.1.102 (Reply)
Apple_96:23:3a     Broadcast          ARP       106     Gratuitous ARP for 192.168.1.102 (Request) (duplicate use of 192.168.1.102 detected!)
```

When the Apple computer sees the Gratuitous ARP asking about its own address, it sends back a "`192.168.1.102 is at 00:23:32:96:23:3a`" and then the system is able to detect a "duplicate IP address" error. This simple process ensures that every IP address on a network segment is unique.

ARP Command

The `arp` command gives you the ability to view a machine's ARP table, showing you which IP addresses are resolved to which physical (MAC) address. Typing `arp -a` in Windows or on a Mac will show you the current ARP cache. Here's an excerpt from a Windows example from a small network:

```
C:\>arp -a

Interface: 192.168.1.101 --- 0x2
  Internet Address      Physical Address      Type
  192.168.1.1           00-18-f8-7e-98-3e     dynamic
  192.168.1.100         00-0c-ce-6d-d2-fc     dynamic
  192.168.1.102         00-09-5c-1c-cd-78     dynamic
  192.168.1.107         00-0f-35-ae-18-52     dynamic
```

It's also possible, using the ARP command, to clear the arp cache, remove specific computers, and so on. Type `arp` with no arguments to get a complete list of possibilities.

PORTS

While IP can provide a unique address for a specific host on a network, a single machine could have multiple, separate software processes running on a single host, each of them communicating simultaneously and separately with other machines on the network. For example, you might use your computer to surf the Web while in the background an e-mail program checks for e-mail, and another process simultaneously downloads a podcast. Allowing this type of operation is the role of **ports**, which are simply identifying numbers assigned to particular software processes. Ports can be either formally defined or configurable; a **socket** in networking terminology is the combination of an IP address and a port number.

The port number is embedded in messaging header information to further steer a particular packet and is used in both TCP and UDP. In the example above, your machine would be using (in addition to dozens of others) port 80 for the Web browser running HTTP, while in the background your e-mail client uses port 143. Port numbers are typically in one of three ranges: "Well known" ports, which are registered with the Internet Assigned Numbers Authority (IANA), run in the range between 0 and 1023; "registered" ports, which are also assigned by the IANA, go from 1024 through 49151; and finally, port numbers ranging from 49152 through 65535 are called "dynamic" or private.

IPV6

The 4,294,967,296 unique addresses offered by 32-bit Internet Protocol Version 4 (IPv4) seemed like at lot when the Internet was being developed. However, with the proliferation of so many connected devices (even your smartphone needs an IP address to browse the Web or send and receive e-mail) the last blocks of unique IPv4 addresses were handed out in January 2011, and the Internet is only able to continue on through recovery of previously allocated addresses, and techniques like Network Address Translation (NAT, page 75).

IP Version Six (**IPv6**)[8] uses 128 bit addresses, which gives us 340,282,366,920, 938,463,463,374,607,431,768,211,456 unique numbers. That's 340 undecillion, 282 decillion, 366 nonillion, 920 octillion, 938 septillion, 463 sextillion, 463 quintillion, 374 quadrillion, 607 trillion, 431 billion, 768 million, 211 thousand and 456 unique addresses.[9] That is something like 4 billion addresses for every living human.

While IPv4 is going to be around for a long time to come, as of this writing, IPv6 has gained some acceptance in show networks, so it's good to at least have a basic understanding of this updated protocol.

---

8   IPv5 was the "Internet Stream Protocol" that offered a different service, not expanded address space.

9   https://www.pingdom.com/blog/the-number-of-possible-ipv6-addresses-read-out-loud/.

A New Address Format and Shorthand

With so many address bits in IPv6, using IPv4's "dot-decimal" scheme would become unwieldy, needing 16 decimal numbers. Instead, the designers of IPv6 use 32 hex[10] digits, broken down into eight "quartets" separated by colons; this approach is called **colon-hexadecimal**.

For example, here's an IPv6 address used by Google[11] for their public DNS service:

2001:4860:4860:0000:0000:0000:0000:8888

To make the number a bit more manageable, leading zeros can be discarded, and any quartet of contiguous zeros can be replaced by a single 0, so this address could also be represented as:

2001:4860:4860:0:0:0:0:8888

To make it even shorter, when contiguous *quartets* of zeros take place in the address, that whole block can be replaced by double colon :: nomenclature, which just means "some number of 0000 quartets":

2001:4860:4860::8888

But what if you had an address like this, with multiple noncontiguous quartets of continuous zeros?

2002:0000:0000:7003:0000:0000:0000:0070

The :: can be used only once in any IPv6 address; using two would be ambiguous), so this address could be shown as either:

2002::7003:0:0:0:70

or

2002:0:0:7003::70

---

10 See "Appendix: Numbering Systems" on page 115 for an explanation of hexadecimal numbering.

11 Facebook found a clever IPv6 address: 2a03:2880:f003:c07:face:b00c::2

54 • CHAPTER 3: NETWORK OPERATIONS

Prefix/Subnet
In the same way that IPv4 addresses have a subnet mask, IPv6 addresses also break down using a variable "prefix" length. For example, if you see a IPv6 address with a /64 prefix length, that would mean that the first 64 bits of the IPv6 address are the network prefix, with the remaining 64 out of the 128 available bits to be assigned to hosts.

The Internet Corporation for Assigned Names and Numbers (ICANN) assigns a "registry prefix" to one of several regional authorities, who then assign addresses to an Internet Service Provider (ISP); a company or organization that wants IPv6 addresses then can get a prefix group from their ISP. A large organization, who could need a massive number of host addresses, can then—just as in IPv4—"borrow" some of the host bits to form subnets. The last part of the host address is called the "interface ID," and is a unique ID in the subnet, typically created by splitting the Ethernet MAC address and inserting a special hex string in the middle: FFFE. This process now gives each IPv6 address a regional location, an ISP, an organization, and an ID for the host, and that all makes a globally unique address like this:

Registry Prefix	ISP Prefix	Customer Prefix	Subnet Prefix	Interface (Host) ID

With this prefix structure, IPv6 replaces the several ranges of classful, IPv4 non-routeable, or private addresses with **Unique Local Addresses** (ULA) and a prefix of fc00::/7. In addition, prefix ff00::/8 has been designated for multicasting, and IPv6 also reserves fe80::/10 for link-local addresses.

Three Types of Transmission
Like any network, IPv6 networks have to accomplish various things for different purposes, and they have three general types of messages: Global Unicast, Multicast, and Anycast.

Global Unicast
There are so many addresses available in IPv6 that it's possible to have completely unique "global unicast" addresses that allow direct communication from one host to another across the Internet. For this purpose, IPv6 reserves addresses whose first quartet starts with 001 (indicated in IPv6 addressing shorthand as

`2000::/3`) for global unicasting. (Put another way, the only options for this quartet would be `0010` and `0011`, or 2 or 3 in hex, which is why all the IPv6 addresses I've listed so far start with 2).

Multicast

Because you can now have direct, NAT-free global unicasting, broadcasting doesn't make much sense anymore; it's been replaced with multicasting.

Anycast

This type of transmission allows multiple servers to use the same unicast address; this would be especially useful in a large network infrastructure where traffic loads need to be balanced across many servers.

IPv6 Network Systems

As in IPv4, IPv6 systems can still use static IP addresses for critical infrastructure like routers or default gateways, and hosts can still use a Dynamic Host Configuration Protocol (DHCP) server for automatic address assignment (however, because the broadcast address has been eliminated, DHCP in IPv6 uses a special multicast address of `FF02::1:2`).

IPv4's Address Resolution Protocol (ARP) uses broadcast transmission, and has been replaced in IPv6 with the **Neighbor Discovery Protocol** (NDP), which can allow a device to discover the local network's IPv6 prefix through some special multicast messages. NDP can also be used to find the address of a Domain Name System (DNS, see page 75) connection for translating text-based names into IP addresses, and a default gateway to know where to send packets going outside the network.

IPv6 in Show Networking?

IPv6 offers some tremendous advantages to the structure of the Internet and has seen some adoption, especially in very large systems. However, IPv4 works just fine for many show networking applications, and with its gigantic installed base, it will be with us for some time to come. And for many of the small, closed networks we are building in our industry (as of this writing in 2020, anyway), IPv6 solves many problems that we don't have. Time will tell...

WHY IP NETWORKING IS GOOD FOR OUR INDUSTRY

The entertainment technology industry has long adapted technologies from bigger, better-funded industries, and the rise of the network is yet another example of this process over the last several decades. As detailed in the last chapter, Ethernet—especially in its switched, full-duplex form—provides us a fast, robust hardware interconnection for all kinds of devices on a show. And building on that layer 1 and 2 Ethernet foundation, moving up through the layer stack into layers 3 and 4, IP-based networking provides us a number of additional benefits:

- Open standard
- Low cost
- Extremely adaptable address space
- Extremely scalable address space
- Tremendous room for expansion and development
- Platform for the future (IPv6 where/when needed)

Chapter 4

MORE NETWORK OPERATIONS

To make efficient and robust networks it's helpful to really understand what's going on inside; let's take a deeper dive. Again—unfortunately—these topics are extremely abstract, since they are literally not viewable.

VISUALIZING TRAFFIC FLOW

Let's start by taking a look at the traffic flow around a simple network that connects hosts using a couple switches, an old hub (obsolete but included here to illustrate some issues), and a router. Also note that the connected devices are depicted here as generic computers, but they could be lighting or sound consoles, machinery control systems, computers running video server software, laser projectors, or just about anything else with an Ethernet jack and an IP address.

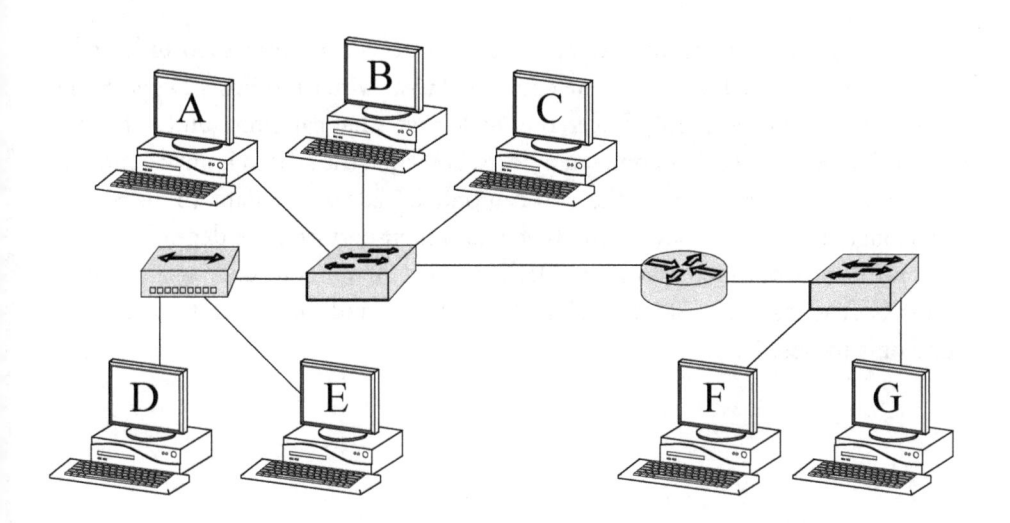

Now let's say that host A wants to unicast a message to host E:

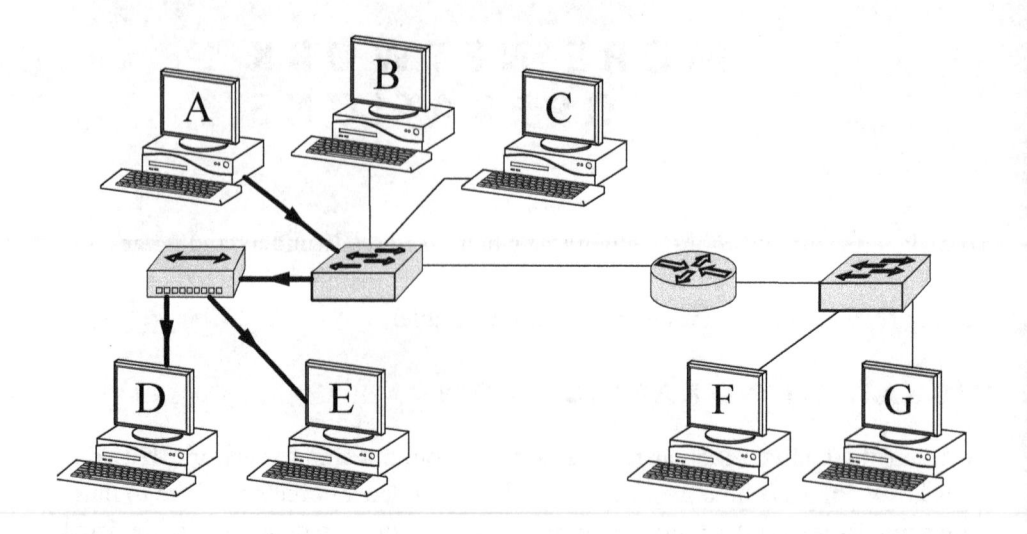

This message was unicast only to E, so why is a copy also forwarded to host D, but not hosts B or C? Hosts A-C are connected to a switch, but hosts D and E are connected to a hub—a dumb, Layer 1-only device—that can only send out every received frame[1] to the other connected hosts. So, while the switch is smart enough to forward to a specific target, the hub can only broadcast the data. (This is why we no longer use hubs—they are inefficient and their performance degrades as the load on the network increases.) Now let's say host A wants to unicast a message to host C. It sends the message out its Ethernet port, and the switch forwards the frame only to host C:

---

[1] Remember, Ethernet operates only at layer 2, and layer 2 carries frames. The units of data at layer 3 are packets..

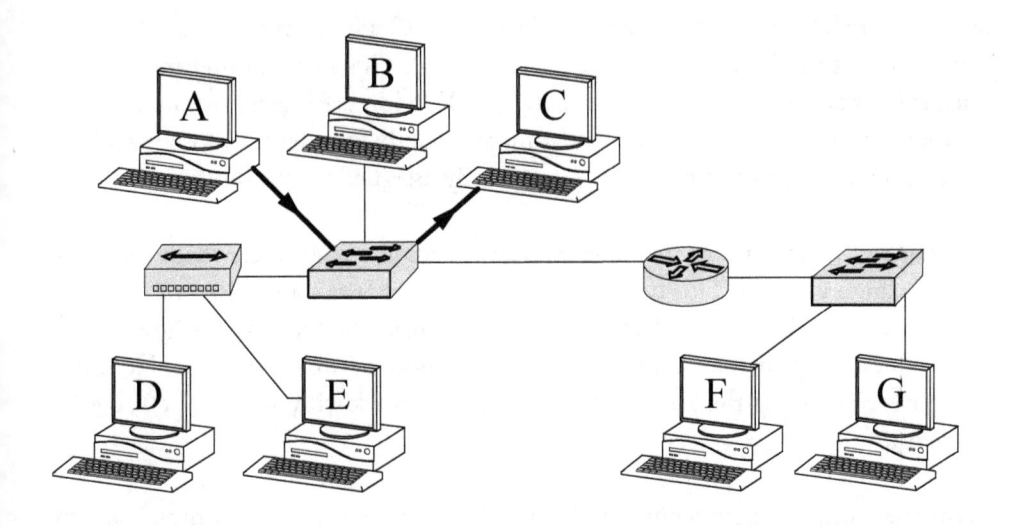

But how does this process actually work? How does the switch really know where to forward the frame? Before answering that question, let's complete the network configuration.

Remember that Ethernet only operates up to Layer 2, and moves its traffic around using fixed, factory-assigned MAC addresses. But in order to make the network useful to higher-level processes (and, therefore, to us), we need to assign Layer 3 IP addresses and subnet masks.

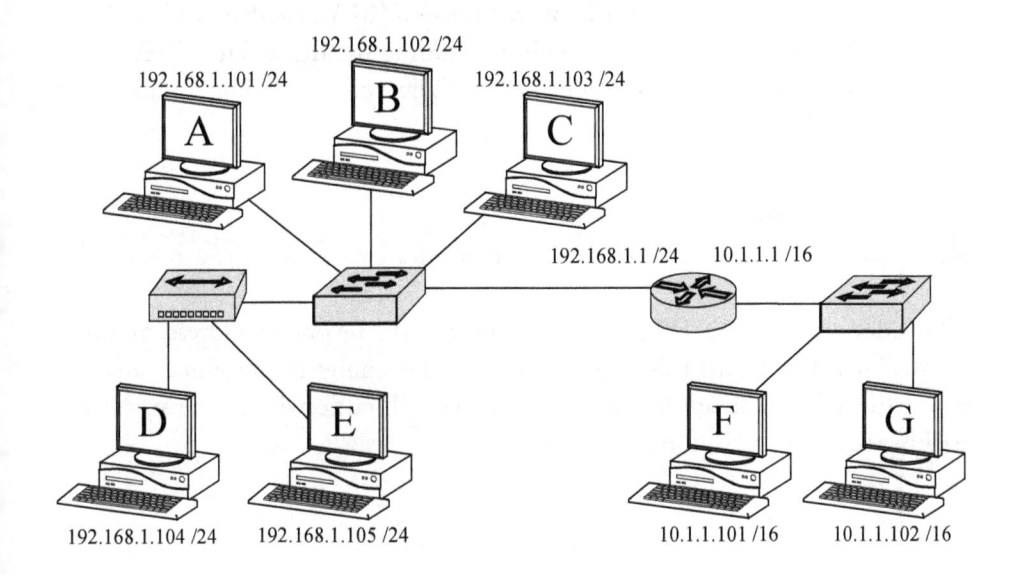

We can see here that on the left side of the block diagram, we have one network with five machines (A-E) assigned private class C addresses (`192.168.1.x`), and a subnet mask of `/24` (`255.255.255.0`). This means, using our simplified subnet approach, the first three octets of the address of each host on this network (in this case `192.168.1`) must match exactly in order for those machines to communicate; all five machines are correctly assigned to this subnet.

On the right hand side of the diagram near the middle is a router, which connects to a separate network. This network is using private class A addresses in the range of `10.1.1.x/16`. Notice that the router itself has two addresses assigned to it, and remember that routers are designed to connect networks together. Here the router is connecting the `192.168.1.0/24`[2] network with the `10.1.0.0/16` network.

Our network is now configured, and host A has an IP address set to `192.168.1.101`; host C is at `192.168.1.103`. We just turned the system on and no traffic has been passed, so let's initiate the process of unicasting from A to C we mentioned above.

RESOLVING LAYER 2 AND 3 ADDRESSES

Host A now has gotten the target IP address of host C (from a human or automated process), but it doesn't yet know the *physical* (MAC) address of host C, so the Layer 2 network can't yet proceed in forwarding the frame. How does it find it? It sends an ARP command out over its Ethernet connection, asking "who has `192.168.1.103`":

```
Source              Destination         Protocol  Length  Info
DellEsgP_88:e7:b6   Broadcast           ARP       106     who has 192.168.1.103?  Tell 192.168.1.101
DellEsgP_88:e8:50   DellEsgP_88:e7:b6   ARP       106     192.168.1.103 is at 00:0b:db:88:e8:50
```

Where does it send it? ARP messages are sent to the broadcast address, meaning the switch will forward this message to all other connected machines, and, of course, the hub will broadcast the frame as it does all traffic, with these two devices reaching this network's "broadcast domain".

---

2 The 0 address is often referred to as the network ID and is what is configured into the router to identify the connected network.

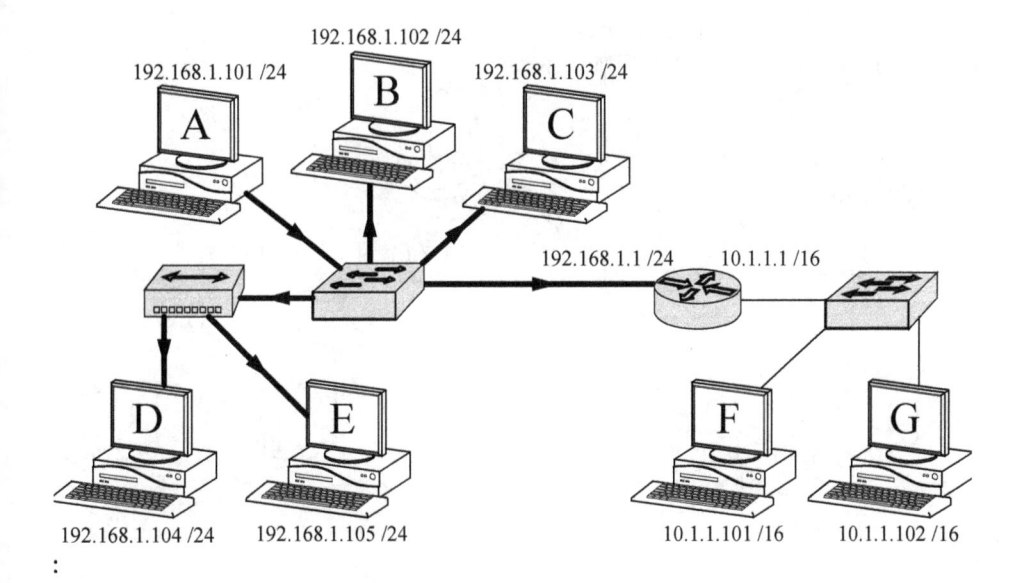

Broadcast Domain

What is a **broadcast domain**? It's simply a part of a network (or all of a smaller network) where all the connected nodes in the domain can reach each other using broadcast messages and Layer 2 communications. But notice that this broadcast domain only includes the machines on the left side of the diagram—those connected to the switch and the hub. Why don't the hosts on the 10.1.1.0 network see the broadcast? Because routers do not forward broadcast messages, and for good reason. Can you imagine if every machine on the Internet got all the broadcast transmissions from every other machine in the world? Segmenting the network in this way is important for management of traffic, security, and maximizing bandwidth utilization, but also requires Layer 3 techniques to forward traffic between the networks. More on that shortly.

Learning MAC Addresses

Back to our example. Host C (like every node in the broadcast domain) receives the broadcast ARP message and replies to Host A's Layer 2 MAC address, which it found contained in the original "who has" ARP message:

INTRODUCTION TO SHOW NETWORKING • 63

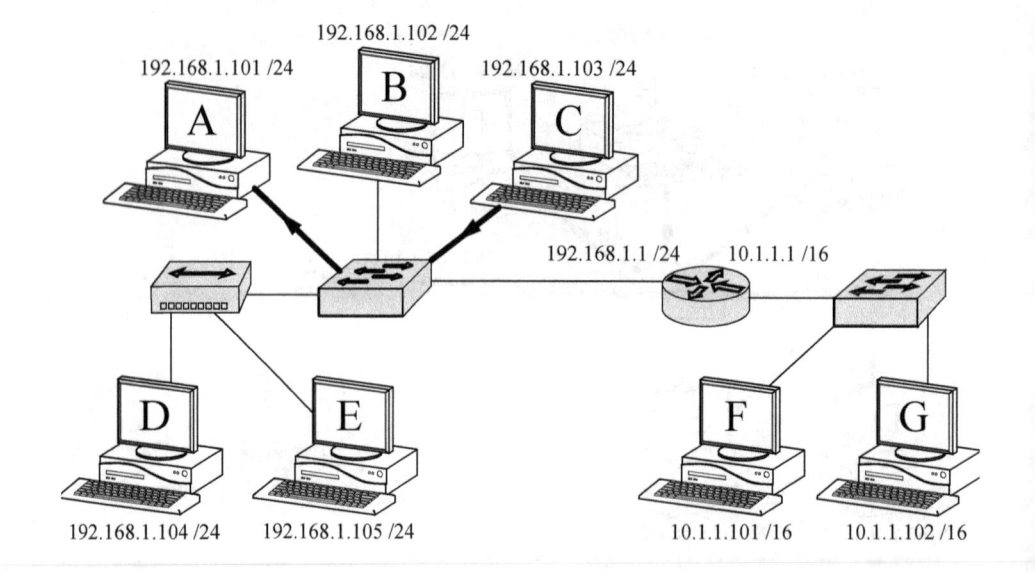

The diagram shows the response from host C being forwarded by the switch only to host A, and not to any of the other connected devices. How does the switch know only to send this message to the interface connected to host A?

Remember, while we've been talking here about Layer 3 IP addresses, the switch doesn't know or care about IP addresses—it's been working with only Layer 2 MAC addresses the entire time. When the initial "Who has" ARP command was issued by host A, the switch was able to read host A's source MAC address, and associate it with a specific physical switch interface; and that's where it forwards host C's unicast response. Additionally, watching this exchange, the switch can now associate host C's MAC address with its related physical interface, and so on.

Host A now receives the ARP response from host C, and since host C's physical, hard-coded MAC address is included in the message, host A can make an ARP table entry associating `192.168.1.103` with host C's MAC address, and now it can send out the message it wanted to send all along (Note: the whole process described above typically happens within milliseconds).

NETWORK TOPOLOGY ISSUES

While show networks can get very complicated and complex, many show networks can be built by following some simple rules. With unmanaged switches and straightforward, closed, show networks, there are basically just two rules you have to follow to make a network:

1. No copper cable runs longer than 100 meters[3]. (If you need more distance, run fiber.)
2. No loops or redundant pathways between switches.

Why no loops? Remember, a switch only has three options for any incoming frame: it can forward the frame on to another interface based on its Layer 2 destination address; it can filter the frame if it's not intended for a particular interface, or it can flood the frame to every interface except the one on which the frame arrived, to keep the frame from bouncing back and forth between two switches. This all works great until someone creates a loop in the network, overriding this safeguard. How does this happen? Let's look at an example.

Broadcast Storms

A new, eager show tech puts together a network made up of two unmanaged switches, A and B, which connect a video controller (host A in the diagram) at front of house to a backstage media server (host B). The technician got the system working with a single connection cable between the switches, and then powers down and heads home for the night. The next day, the tech has the idea that running a second cable between the switches would give redundancy and double the bandwidth, which would be especially useful when transferring large media files between the two systems. So the tech runs a second, redundant cable from switch A to switch B, and powers up the system. Even though in our business we like redundancy, in this case, by running the second cable, the well-meaning technician set the stage for a broadcast storm. Let's work through the situation to understand why.

On power up, host A, the video controller, attempts to connect with host B, the media server. The host B media server Layer 3 IP address had been manually configured into the video controller during setup, but the Layer 2 Ethernet network needs the physical MAC address to operate, so the operating system of host A sends out a broadcast ARP message. Switch A then floods this broadcast frame to every other interface (except, of course, the interface that delivered the message), and because there are two connections between the switches, switch B now receives two identical, incoming broadcast ARP request messages (two copies of the frame indicated by different line styles in the diagram):

---

3 Some higher performance networks have shorter maximum run lengths.

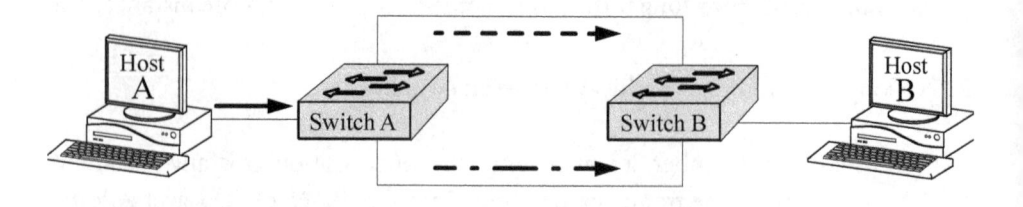

Since it's a broadcast message, switch B does the only thing it knows to do: it floods both broadcast frames:

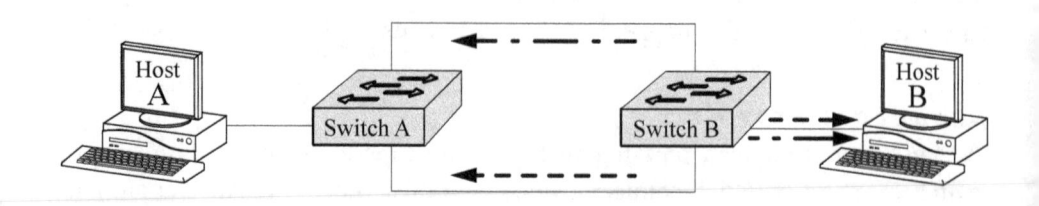

One of those interfaces is connected to the media server host B, which will receive both ARP requests and likely just respond twice. But what about the connections heading back to switch A? The switch, as we discussed, is smart enough not to return frames back to the incoming interface, but because we got two frames on *different* interfaces, switch B sends the frame that arrived on the top connection in the diagram out to the bottom connection, and vice versa:

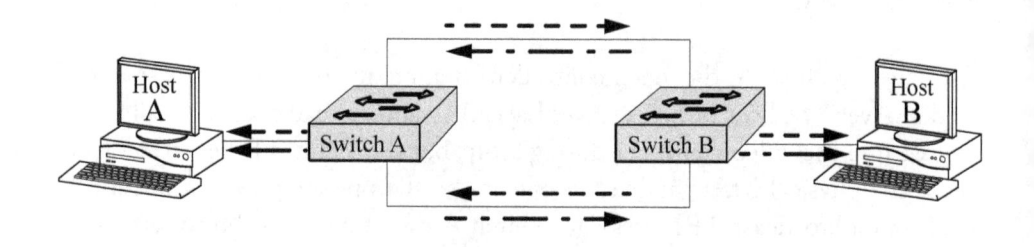

Switch A now sees two broadcast frames coming in on two interfaces, so it takes the frame coming in on the top connection and as part of its flood sends it to the bottom connection in the diagram, closing the loop back to Switch B, and vice versa. This is called a **broadcast storm**, and the frames likely will end up looping around the system until one of the duplicate pathways is disconnected, typically overloading the network to the point that it will stop functioning. To avoid broadcast storms in simple systems, loops and redundant pathways must be avoided.

Managing Loops

In our show-must-go-on industry, we often want redundancy, so how could we implement it in a network? There are two primary protocols implemented in many managed switches.

The first is the **Spanning Tree Protocol** (STP). STP learns the topology of the system and is able to manage the system so it remains loop free. The problem with STP for our fast-paced work environment is that STP can take some time to "converge" after the network topology is changed, either intentionally or through a failure. The Rapid Spanning Tree Protocol (RSTP) speeds up this process, and can "converge" a network within a few seconds, meaning that we can actually use it to our advantage to manage redundant connections. While the details of STP are beyond our scope here, enabling this feature on many managed switches is often a matter of simply checking a box on a management interface.

Another approach for managing a fault-tolerant network topology is **Ethernet Automatic Protection Switching** (EAPS). which is primarily intended as a way to manage rings in Ethernet networks, and you might find it implemented in some switches. EAPS is implemented in a "domain," and each domain has a single main node and one or more "transit nodes." When a failure occurs in the network, any devices that detect the fault notify the system; which then opens up the secondary port and lets the system know to update their forwarding information. This approach can be very responsive and update the network topology very quickly.

Virtual LANs (VLAN)

It's often good network design to separate different types of traffic. For example, let's say on a show, we have lighting and video controllers at front of house; backstage we need two lighting data distributor units, and two video display servers. Probably the simplest approach would be to get two sets of switches and physically separate the networks, and using good networking practices (more in "Show Networking Best Practices" on page 77) we coordinate between the two departments and have each one use a different set of IP addresses.

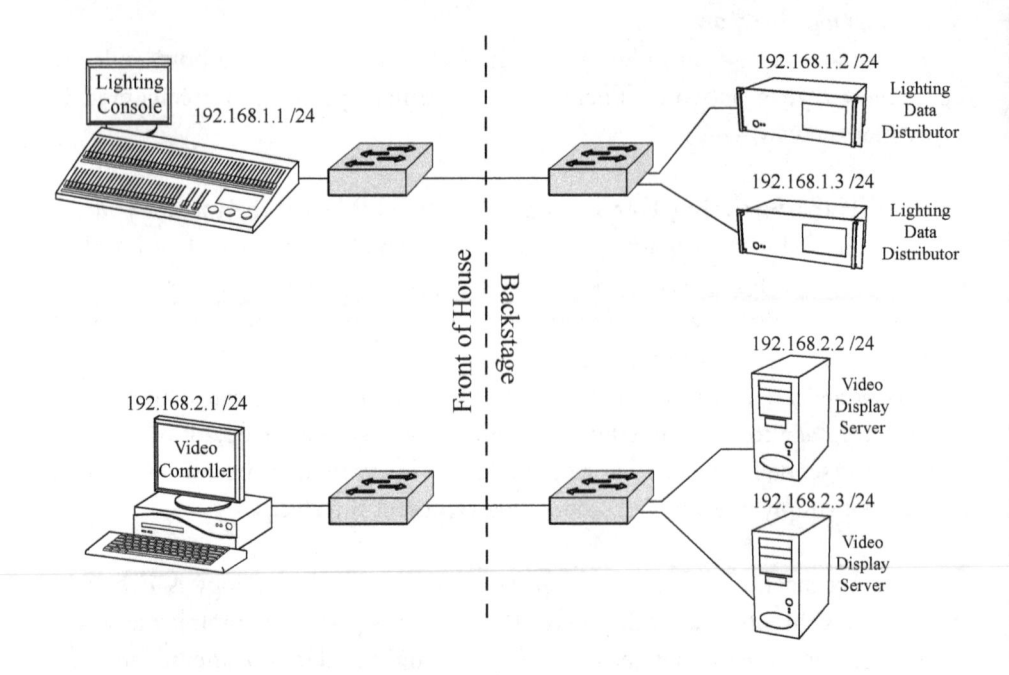

We now have two physically separate broadcast domains, meaning the video system will never see the lighting traffic:

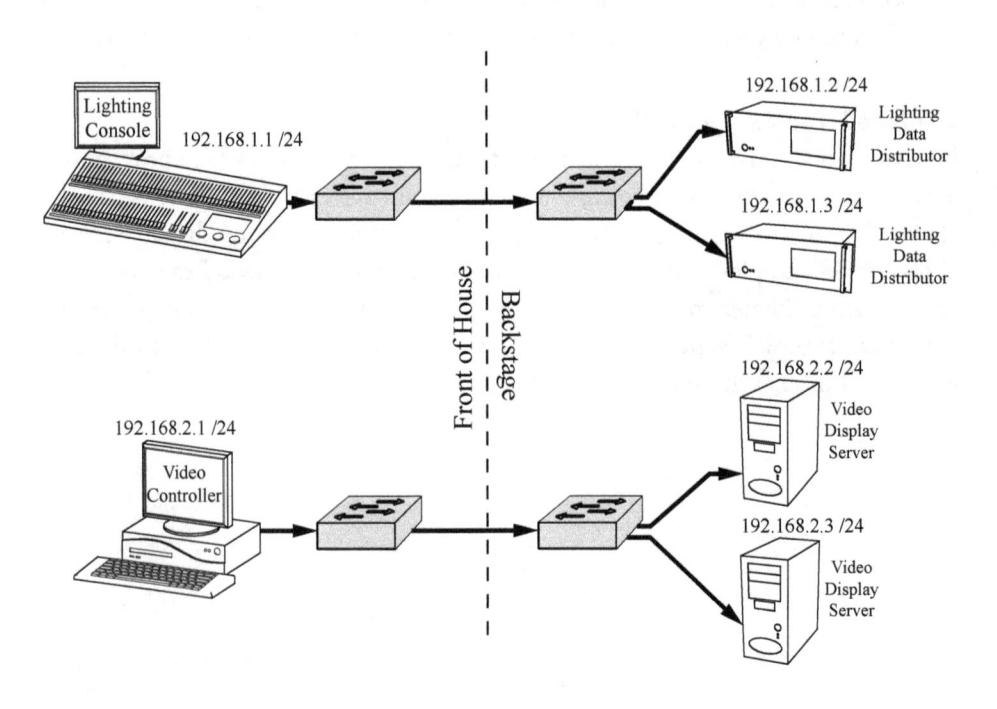

68 • **CHAPTER 4: MORE NETWORK OPERATIONS**

With this design, we need to purchase four switches, and manage two sets of cables, etc. But relative to the cost of these systems, switches aren't all that expensive, and we are very good at cable management in our industry, so this isn't hard to do. This approach gives us some redundancy (always a good thing)—if there is a problem in the lighting network, the video network will remain unaffected.

Let's look at another possible approach, putting all the connected devices onto a single physical network:

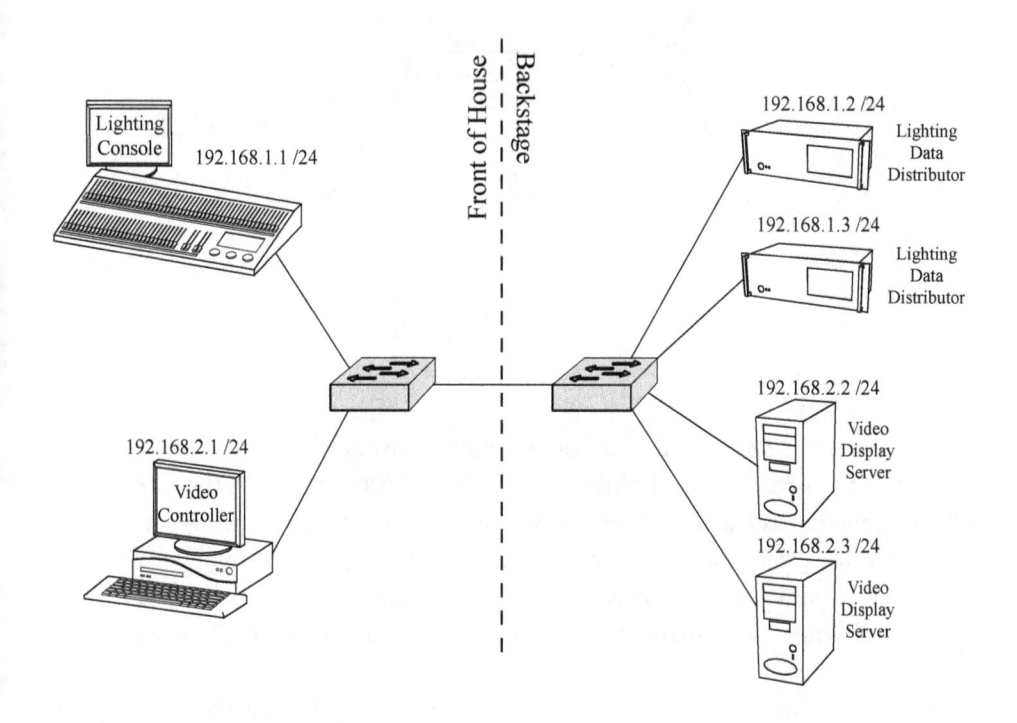

Take a look at the IP addresses. Because we used good networking practices in building our network, lighting is on one subnet, video is on another. Under normal circumstances, lighting won't be able to communicate with the video machines, and vice versa. But what if a machine gets mis-addressed? Or what if one of the systems has some other problem? And what about the broadcast domain?

INTRODUCTION TO SHOW NETWORKING • 69

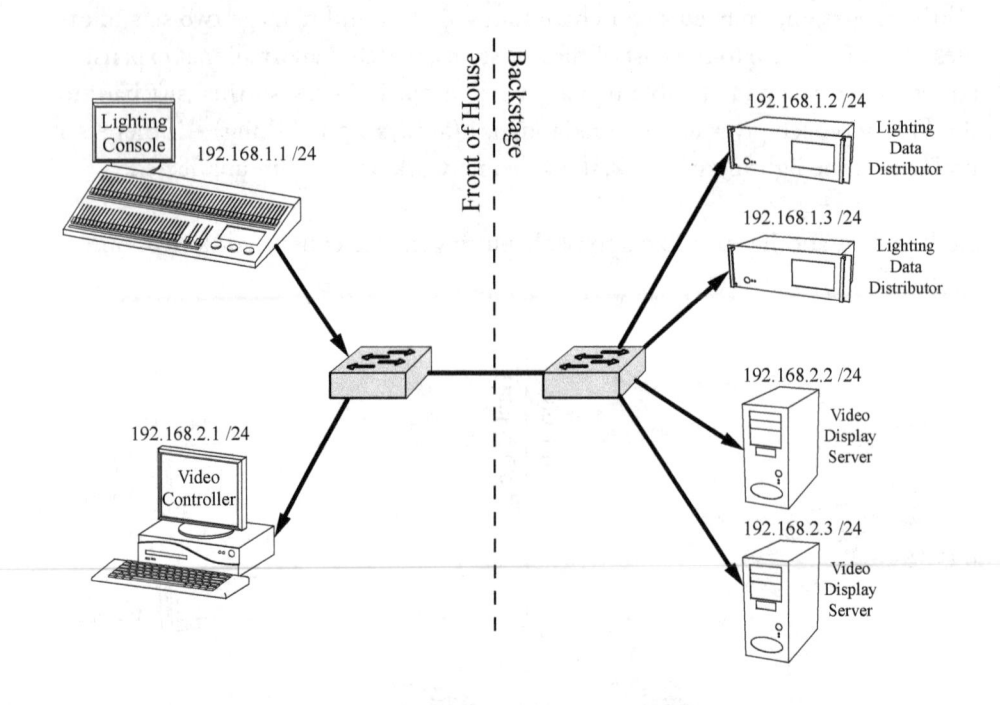

In this case, with all the devices on a single network, they all share the same broadcast domain. So if the lighting console broadcasts a message, the receivers in all the video devices will then have to process each broadcast lighting data frame, wasting time, even though the data was never intended for those units. What if, instead, we could still use a shared physical infrastructure—saving hardware costs and simplifying system management—but separate the networks virtually?

Separating networks virtually while sharing common physical resources is the role of the **Virtual Local Area Network** (VLAN). VLANs are available as a feature in many managed switches, and most show-oriented switches feature very easy VLAN configuration. These systems use the hardware of the switch itself to separate all the connected devices in each VLAN into their own *virtually* separated broadcast domain. With the cost-effective switching horsepower we have available, this approach allows a single physical network to simultaneously serve a number of purposes, while unifying cable management and configuration, or letting us do things like share long haul, high bandwidth fiber links:

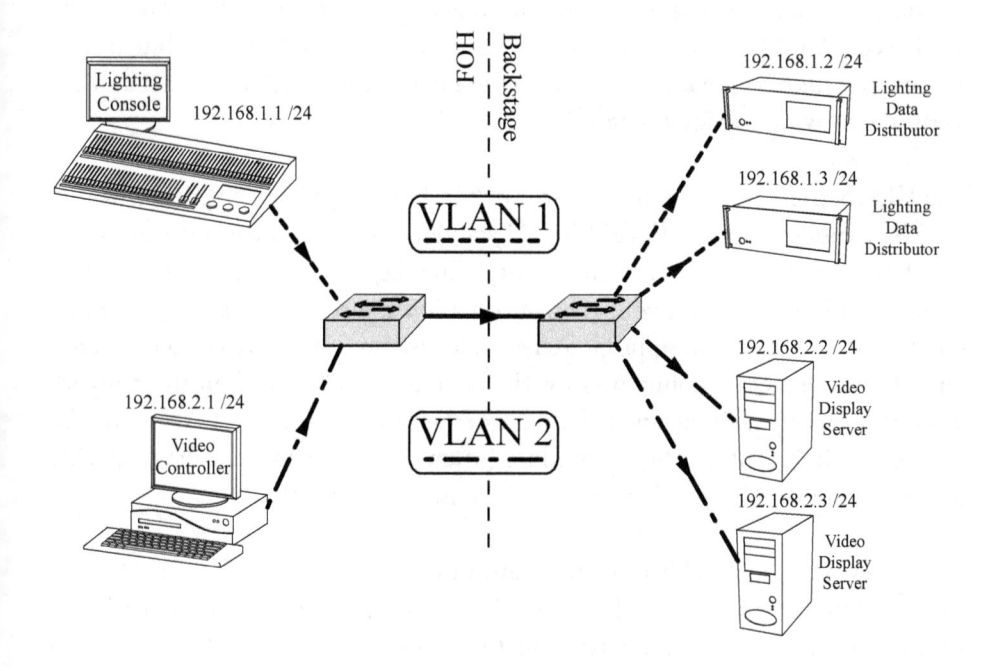

With this VLAN system, we effectively have two separate networks, each with its own broadcast domains:

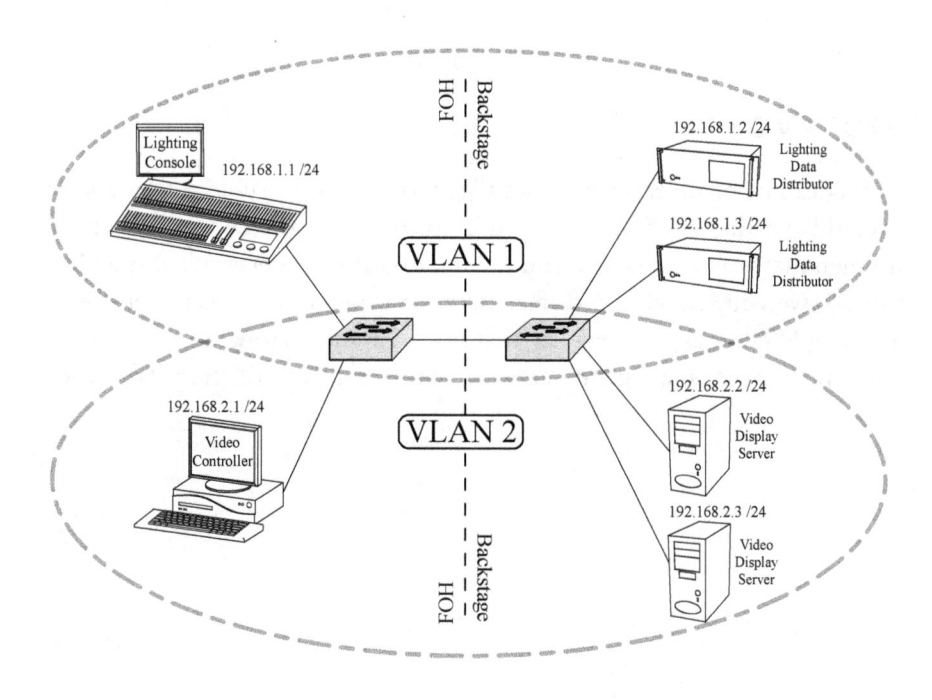

INTRODUCTION TO SHOW NETWORKING • 71

Of course, we need to make sure that the connection line between the two switches—called a VLAN trunk—has enough bandwidth to handle the combined traffic, but with high bandwidth switches this is a manageable problem (especially for control data, which is not as bandwidth intensive).

The VLAN traffic is sorted out in most networks by "tagging" the packets with a VLAN number, using the IEEE 802.1Q standard; un-tagged packets run on the switch system's "native" VLAN. So the trunk line shown above would carry tagged traffic from both VLANs; with that information the receiving switch would be able to sort out the traffic appropriately. Typically, physical interfaces on switches come from the factory configured for the default VLAN, and then the network administrator sets each specific Ethernet interface to a particular VLAN using the managed switch configuration procedure (often a web page or in a show-specific switch, a front panel control) software of the managed switch.

One other note on VLANs: Switch hardware works at Layer 2 to implement VLANs, but it's good networking practice to put all the hosts in a particular VLAN into their own Layer 3 IP subnet (as shown in the example above). On some managed, multi-layer switches, it's even possible to route between VLANs containing different subnets (see "Example Managed Show Control Network" on page 99).

ROUTING

Routing can be complex; entire books are written on the subject. Routers are not (as of this writing in 2020) widely used in our industry, but they offer powerful functionality when needed, and are important to understand, at least in basic terms, so we will scratch the surface here. To explore the concept, let's return to our example network, and let's say that host A wants to send a packet to host G, which we know is on a separate network with completely different IP addresses:

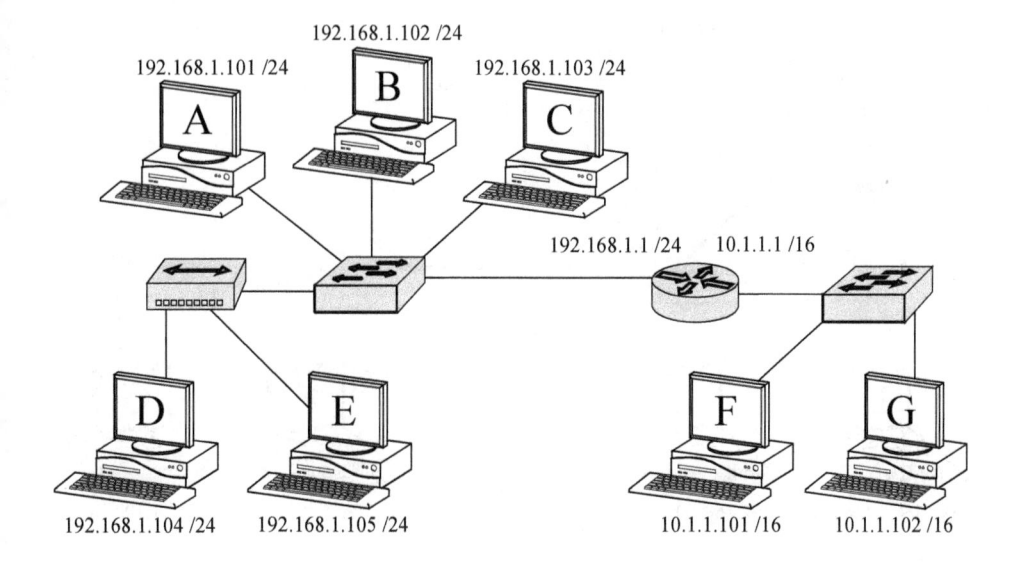

[Network diagram showing hosts A (192.168.1.101/24), B (192.168.1.102/24), C (192.168.1.103/24) connected via switches to a router with interfaces 192.168.1.1/24 and 10.1.1.1/16, and hosts D (192.168.1.104/24), E (192.168.1.105/24), F (10.1.1.101/16), G (10.1.1.102/16).]

In this simplified example network, the router has two physical Ethernet interfaces[4], with one connected to each network, and each interface assigned an appropriate IP address/subnet mask within that network. The router keeps a **routing table** telling it where to find (in this case, by physical interface) each network. When the packet comes in on the `192.168.1.1` interface destined for `10.1.1.102`, the router looks in its routing table and then it knows to which interface to forward the packet.

But how do the connected hosts send packets to the router? Through the use of a **default gateway** (or "router address" on a macOS machine), which is simply the IP address to which a host will forward packets for which it can't otherwise find a delivery route—typically that means an address outside of our local subnet. In this case, the gateway out of our `192.168.1.0` network is `192.168.1.1`, which has been assigned to an interface on the router by a network administrator. So, when host A (`192.168.1.101`) attempts to send a message to host G at `10.1.1.102`, the sending machine will immediately realize that this address is not reachable within its subnet, and it will instead send the message to its default Gateway of `192.168.1.1`; sending the packet to the default gateway sends it to the router.

---

4   Routers can exist as software of other devices like multi-layer switches, and, therefore, would not have multiple, physical interfaces, but the physical interface approach is easier to visualize so I'm using it here.

INTRODUCTION TO SHOW NETWORKING • 73

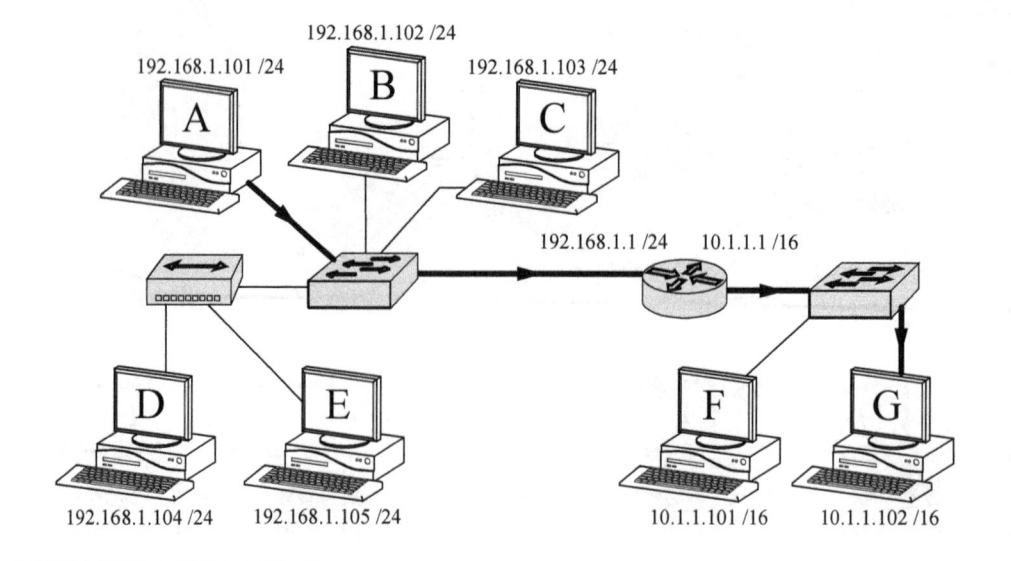

In this case, the message from A to G was sent using TCP, so host G now has to acknowledge the TCP transaction back to `192.168.1.101`. But it knows that this target IP address is outside its network, so where does it send it? To its own default gateway for the `10.1.0.0` network: `10.1.1.1`. When it receives the packet, the router looks at the `192.168.1.x` destination address, checks its routing table, and forwards the packet back to the appropriate interface; the connected network then delivers it.

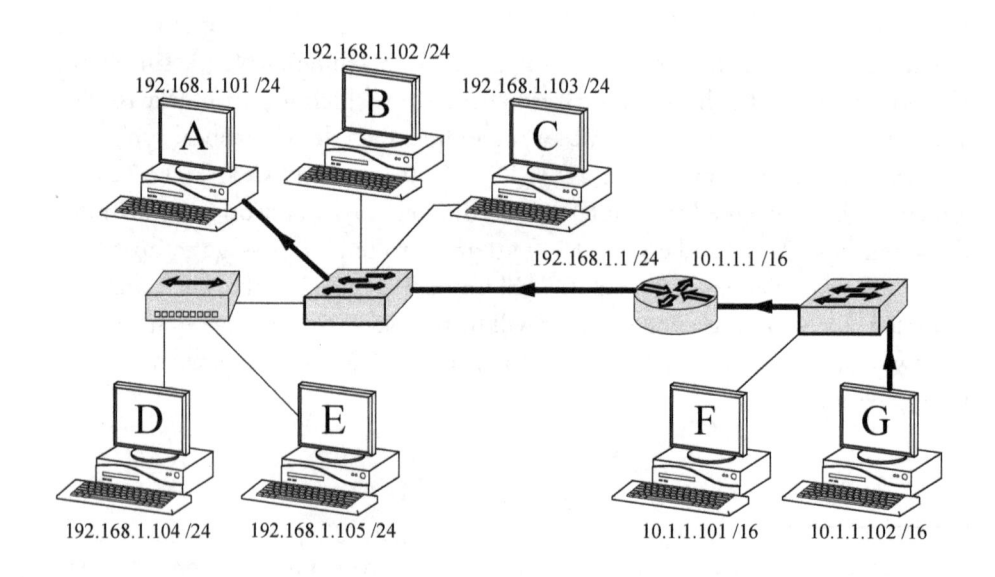

Keep in mind that Layer 2 switches don't understand the IP addresses, operate at a low level, and work very fast. Routers, with all the processing they have to do, are inevitably a bit slower (although still very fast!); this is something to keep in mind when designing your network. For a further example of a real-world router usage on a show, see "Routers" on page 28.

OTHER NETWORK SYSTEM PROTOCOLS

As of this writing in 2020, most show networks are small, unmanaged, and not connected to larger networks or to the Internet. But since our networks get more sophisticated all the time, it's important to understand some of the issues involved in—and techniques and systems used in—larger networks, so I'll offer a brief overview here.

Internet Group Management Protocol (IGMP)

Some traffic on a show network may use multicasting to efficiently transmit data out from a single device to multiple other devices; the multicast subscription process uses a protocol called **Internet Group Management Protocol** (IGMP) that operates at Layer 3. However, a layer 2 switch can't understand IGMP and so in order to ensure delivery, its only option would be to flood (broadcast) all the multicast packets to every connected device; this, however, negates any of the traffic management benefits of multicasting. To deal with this, **IGMP Snooping** was developed, which can "snoop" into the Layer 3 IGMP traffic to determine whether or not a particular connected interface on the switch should receive multicast traffic. In this way, a switch can maintain the efficiency of the multicast approach, delivering traffic only to interfaces which need it.

Domain Name System (DNS)

In show networks, we (as of this writing in 2020, anyway) rarely use the **Domain Name System** (DNS), but it is a critical part of the Internet, so it's worth a brief mention here. When you type a Universal Resource Locator (URL), such as http://www.controlgeek.net/ into your Web browser, it submits the name to the DNS, which then returns the IP address of the text-based name. Packets can then be routed to the correct IP address.

Network Address Translation (NAT)

Another technique that is rarely used in show networking (in 2020, anyway) but widely used in home and office networking is **Network Address Translation** (NAT). Using NAT, a router (like the one you likely have at home) connecting a LAN (like your home network) to the Internet changes the source and/or destination addresses of packets that travel through it, so that a single IP address on your router (typically assigned by your ISP) can be used to connect to the Internet and be shared by many hosts on the private network serviced by the router.

For example, let's say we have a small private network with 10 hosts connected by a router/switch, which assigns private, Class C addresses. If one of the 10 machines needs to communicate with another machine on the private network (e.g., to transfer a sound file from your desktop to the laptop), the machines simply talk directly to each other through the switch. However, if a user wants to browse a favorite Web page, he or she now needs to connect to the Internet, and now the user's machine needs a publicly-reachable IP address in order for its data to travel successfully on the public Internet. So, using NAT, the router changes the source address of the packets from the sending machine to match the publicly reachable IP address of the router. When packets return for the machine running the Web browser, the router also changes the destination of returning packets back to match the private address of the destination host. In this way, many hosts can share a single, precious publicly reachable IP address.

Virtual Private Network (VPN)
In these days where security is a primary concern, a **Virtual Private Network** (VPN) offers users a way to use the public, insecure Internet to access their own (or other) secure networks. Traffic on a VPN connection is encrypted, and connections to the main system are often through a security firewall. Details of VPNs are also outside our scope here.

Quality of Service (QoS)
Quality of Service (QoS) is very confusingly named. It basically defines levels of performance and prioritization in a network, and can be assigned to a particular user or a type of traffic. It's was designed for things like Voice Over IP (VOIP), which is the backbone of many office and home telephone systems. VOIP packets, for example, typically need a higher priority of service than an e-mail. Not all networks support it, and the details of how QoS works are outside the scope of this book, but it is something that you might see in a sophisticated show network, especially for large scale audio/video transmission applications.

Link Layer Discovery Protocol (LLDP)
The **Link Layer Discovery Protocol** (LLDP) allows network devices to advertise their identity and capabilities to their "neighbors" on an Ethernet switch system, allowing automated discovery and even configuration.

SHOW NETWORKING BEST PRACTICES

Let's pull all this together and close out this section with some entertainment networking best practices. Of course, best practices are constantly evolving; this list started with a panel I chaired at the 2016 North American Theater Engineering and Architecture Conference (NATEAC)[5]. For that panel I got together Kevin Loewen, Engineering Manager at the Pathway Connectivity office of Acuity Brands Lighting and Peter Stepniewicz, Principal Show Electronic Engineer, Walt Disney Imagineering. Kevin Gross, AVA Networks, also gave us valuable feedback, and Scott Blair of Megapixel VR contributed to some later revisions for the 2019 NAMM[6] conference. While this group represents a pretty broad cross section of the industry, including users, manufacturers, and developers, the list just represents the general consensus (as tweaked by me) of the group.

General Network Architecture
- View cable/fiber plant as a flexible infrastructure, which potentially can be used for networking, audio/video distribution, DMX 512, or even analog signals.
- Use wireless only for special use cases where you have no alternative.
- Select show networking protocols that are modern and network-friendly where possible.
- Hire a qualified contractor for permanent installations, or be sure to read and follow specifications and instructions, and performance-test all network links.
- Consider venue/show staff knowledge and support sources when designing your system.
- Choose address assignment by type of gear that will be used.
- Keep in mind that well-designed network/cable infrastructure helps to accommodate future technologies.
- Minimize the number of "switch hops" for high bandwidth data like streaming audio or video (for example if you have three switches and only two devices carrying this kind of media, plug them into the same switch if possible).

Network Hardware
- 1 Gbit/s switches give plenty of bandwidth for most show networking applications today and likely into the near future. 10 Gbit/s and other higher rate connections might be useful or needed for current or future special applications (like video) or high capacity backbones.
- Avoid consumer-grade switches, and consider using managed switches, since

---

5 www.nateac.org

6 www.namm.org

in the context of an show networking system, switches are cheap, and some more advanced features (like Internet Group Management Protocol (IGMP)) available in managed switches are increasingly important in modern systems.
- Consider using switches made for the entertainment industry, since they are better focused on the needs of our market and our users, have accessible support, and are made to be easy to use; enterprise grade IT equipment can be very confusing to setup.
- Consider (more expensive) Power over Ethernet (PoE) switches for some specialized applications like IP surveillance cameras and A/V network devices.
- Consider (more expensive) AVB/TSN/Milan capable switches if running audio equipment that uses it.
- Ensure that Energy-Efficient Ethernet (EEE) can be disabled (or is not implemented) in switches used for audio networks like Audinate Dante.
- Incorporate monitoring ability. Computers are cheap these days.
- Use physically redundant switches or Virtual Local Area Networks (VLAN) to separate traffic. VLANs are very easy to configure with modern entertainment-oriented switches.
- Use small business or enterprise-grade dedicated wireless access points when necessary (and don't use Wi-Fi for real-time control).
- Don't use home grade routers (you don't likely need the router anyway and if you do, you don't want a consumer grade router).

Copper
- Comply with the TIA/EIA-568 structured cabling standard. The B version is more common, but either A or B can be fine if used consistently on a show/venue.
- Cat 5e Unshielded Twisted Pair (UTP) is suitable for Gigabit Ethernet and should be fine for most show networking and many audio transmission applications in North America today and into the near future.
- Cat 6, 6A, 7 and/or Shielded Twisted Pair (STP) may be required or recommended currently or in the future by some manufacturers for specialized (typically high bandwidth) applications.
- Use pre-made patch cables. Large manufacturers make cable so cheap that it's typically not worth crimping your own connectors.
- Keep total Cat 5e segment length under 100m (including patch cables). Cat 6, depending on the use, can have shorter working lengths.
- Heavier duty Neutrik etherCON (and compatible) connectors are available for show purposes.
- Heavier duty (and easier to coil) Cat 5e and other cables are available and made

especially for show purposes.

For permanent copper installations:
- Terminate cable runs to a jack in the wall, then use a patch cord for the short run to the equipment.
- Minimize the patch cable length since these cables are typically lower performance.
- Remember that conduit runs are typically specified by others and can often be longer than you think. 80m is a good target length, 90m maximum to accommodate 5m patch cables on each end.

Fiber
- Fiber is complicated/expensive to terminate and is best for long runs or high bandwidth applications, or where lightning/extreme EMI immunity is needed.
- LC Duplex is the most common fiber connector in our market; you might also see SFP or higher rate SFP+ connectors on networking equipment.
- Single mode fiber is typically needed for very long distances.
- Heavier duty Neutrik opticalCON Duo or Quad ruggedized connectors are available.

Security
- Physical security is very important in our industry and is your first line of network defense.
- Keep in mind that few of our protocols have any intrinsic security.
- Consider not using or restricting access to DHCP servers.
- Use firewalls; start with firewall that is totally closed and open from there.
- Use VPN for remote access.
- Shut down unneeded Wi-Fi (which is very useful for programming, etc.) during the show.
- Keep your network off the Internet. If you have to put it on the internet, limit and constrain access. A useful approach when this is necessary is to have one machine on the show network and use a highly secure external remote access method to that one machine. Then you are virtually in the show network without exposing the whole thing.

A MATURE SOLUTION

Successful standards and technology are pulled into existence; pushing them rarely works. In the early 2020s, networks are more than doing the job on many show networks, and while networking techniques and technology, of course, continually evolve, at this point the core technologies we are using—Ethernet, TCP, UDP, IP—are mature technologies that have been developing since the 1970s. And this is a good thing, since this mature infrastructure means we can now concentrate on telling stories (our main job) and spend less time inventing tools.[7]

---

[7] I've written much more about this on my blog: https://controlgeek.net/blog/2020/8/20/development-and-evolution-of-show-technology-articles-and-timeline

Chapter 5

EXAMPLE NETWORKS

Our audiences demand performance and reliability from our show systems that far exceed their own experience with similar technologies (i.e., cell phones, home networks, etc.), so our "show must go on" industry needs robust networks. At the same time, we have cost pressures, and the physical environment backstage is often not kind: show equipment gets abuse that can exceed what might be found in many factory or military environments (think about dragging networking cabling through the mud after a festival). Given those concerns, my general show system design principles[1] are:

1. Ensure Safety
2. The Show Must Go On (Maximize Reliability)
3. Simpler is Always Better
4. Strive for Elegance
5. Complexity is Inevitable; Convolution is Not
6. Make it Scalable, and Leave Room for Unanticipated Changes
7. Ensure Security

NETWORK DESIGN/IMPLEMENTATION PROCESS

Within that framework, here is the process I use when designing a network; this is my own way of working and not based on any formal standard:

1. Analyze Network Needs
2. Design Address/Subnet Scheme
3. Determine Network Topology
4. Document the Network
5. Build, Label, and Verify the Network
6. Implement Security
7. Maximize Reliability

---

1 These principles are covered in detail in my *Show Networks and Control Systems* book.

Let's go through each step in a bit of detail.

1: Analyze Network Needs

One of my top guiding principles for show system design is "Simpler is always better", and I think for networks this means just to include only what is needed (with room for expansion, of course). To determine this, I usually start with a list of gear that is going to be connected. Then I ask a few other questions:

- What kind of traffic is being carried: Control data and/or media?
- Is routing required?
- Does the system need wireless access?
- What are the network security risks?

2: Design Address/Subnet Scheme

With the list of equipment and various aspects of the network defined, next I determine a scheme for IP addresses, asking these questions:

- How many subnets are required?
- How are IP Addresses assigned? (Is a DHCP server needed?)

3: Determine Network Topology

With all this information in place, I determine the layout of the network, basing the design around the best gear available within the resources, to maximize reliability. And in addition to the answers to previous questions, there are a few more:

- Do we need VLANs?
- Are runs over 100m (about 328 feet) required in the system?
- Is high bandwidth digital audio or video passing through the network?
- Are redundant data pathways required, and if so, how will they be implemented? (STP, EAPS, etc).
- Are managed and/or multi-layer switches required?

4: Document the Network

Networks decouple virtual signal flow pathways from the physical connections, so it's nearly impossible to figure out what's going on in a network simply by looking at the cabling. For these and many other reasons, documentation is critical on show networks. Two primary documents are typical:

- IP Address List: This spreadsheet is the minimum document you need. It should have the name of the connected device, its IP address, and any other

relevant information. If you are using an managed network and VLANs you will also likely need the interface number and VLAN assignment.
- Network diagram: Depending on your experience, the experience level of the network users, and the complexity of the network, you also might want to create a network block diagram.

5: Build, Label, and Verify the Network

Now with the design and documentation done, it's time to build the network! Make sure you follow best practices for running any type of show system (run cables neatly, protect cable runs, etc) and make sure to label everything (but think carefully before putting IP address labels on devices; we'll talk more about this in the next section). Once the network is up and running my process is:

- Double check all cables and labels
- Verify IP addresses
- Ping everything

6: Implement Security

Networking gives us enormous power and flexibility at an affordable price, because we base our systems on the same technologies used widely in offices and factories. That also, however, exposes shows to some security risks. Network security—especially when your system is connected to the Internet (which I try to avoid)—can be a complex moving target. However, there's some basic ideas that will help address security for show networks.

- Keep your network hardware and infrastructure locked up wherever possible. This "physical security" can go a long way in a typically controlled backstage area.
- Keep your network off the Internet if possible. If you must connect it, severely restrict access, use a firewall, and implement a VPN if possible.
- Use WiFi only if needed, and disable when not in use. Use appropriate WiFi security.
- Change default passwords and keep your passwords secure.
- If using standard computers, install only what is needed for the show on the machine.

This is of course an incomplete and simplistic list; entire books have been written on security. But most importantly it's best to considered security from the beginning of a network system design right through to closing night.

7: Maximize Operational Reliability

This is a complex subject, but planning as much as possible for failures and developing back up plans in advance means that if you have a problem, all you have to do is implement your plan.

- What is the backup plan in case of a cable failure?
- What is the backup plan in case of a network hardware failure?

With a basic process in place, let's take a look at some realistic network applications. I haven't mentioned any specific gear in these systems, but all the designs are based on commonly used gear and practices as of this writing in 2020.

EXAMPLE LIGHTING NETWORK

For our first example, let's take a look a lighting system to be installed in a small venue. We want to connect a control console, some dimmers that need DMX512-A, two moving lights, and two LED fixtures. Let's apply my design process:

1: Analyze Network Needs
What kind of traffic is being carried: Control data and/or media?
This is a control only network.

Is routing required?
No

Does the system need wireless access?
Yes, for a wireless phone app which will remotely access the console.

What are the network security risks?
This is a lighting system that doesn't really present any safety risks to crew or performers, so the only real risk of someone accessing the network is messing with the show. This wouldn't be great, but it's not life or death.

2: Design Address/Subnet Scheme
How many subnets are required?
One.

How are IP Addresses assigned? (Is a DHCP server needed?)
This lighting system and its control protocols are capable of using addresses assigned by the console's built-in DHCP server; however, in this case, the production electrician prefers to have everything locked down with fixed addresses.

However, for convenience, the phone running the remote control app will be set to DHCP, and it will get its address from the console.

3: Determine Network Topology
Do we need VLANs?
No.

Are runs over 100m required in the system?
This is a small venue, so the run length from the console to backstage is about 200', and that's well under the 100 meter (approximately 328 feet) limitation.

Is high bandwidth digital audio or video passing through the network?
No, just lighting control data. This, along with the run lengths described above, means that plain old Cat 5e cable should be fine.?

Are redundant data pathways required, and if so, how will they be implemented? (STP, EAPS, etc).
With a single switch, no redundant data pathways are necessary.

Are managed and/or multi-layer switches required?
This system could be built with a cheap unmanaged switch, but in this case the electrician decides to get a switch made for show purposes. It's already optimized for lighting protocols and offers show-oriented support.

4: Document the Network
IP Address List:
The electrician decides to use Class A private ("non-routeable") addresses:

Device	IP Address (Subnet Mask: 255.255.0.0)
Console	10.0.1.11
Phone	10.0.1.x (assigned by DHCP)
Gateway	10.0.1.21
Moving Light 1	10.0.1.31
Moving Light 2	10.0.1.32
LED Light 1	10.0.1.41
LED Light 2	10.0.1.42

Network diagram:

[Network diagram showing: Lighting Console (10.0.1.11) at FOH connected via Ethernet Switch across Stage to Wireless Access Point with WiFi to Phone for Remote Control (Lighting Console App, DHCP); Protocol Gateway (10.0.1.21, 255.255.0.0) with DMX out to Dimmers; LED Light 1 (10.0.1.41, 255.255.0.0), LED Light 2 (10.0.1.42, 255.255.0.0), Moving Light 1 (10.0.1.31, 255.255.0.0), Moving Light 2 (10.0.1.32, 255.255.0.0)]

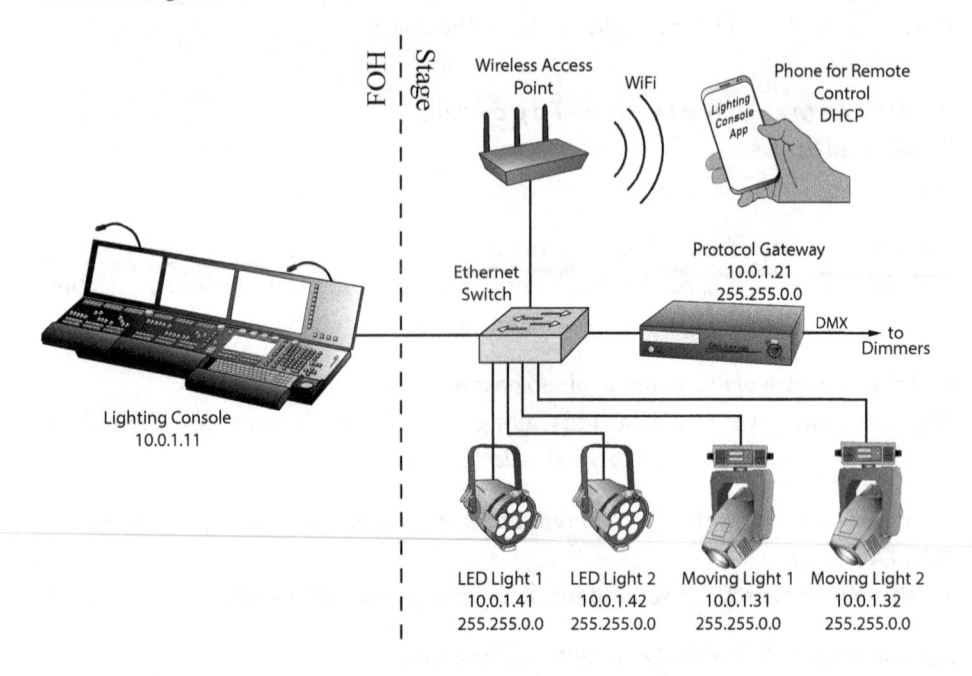

5: Build, Label, and Verify the Network

Double check all cables and labels

The electrician goes through and labels every cable with it's connected to and where it's going.

Verify IP addresses

In this case, connecting the devices to the console also verifies the connection, so when that works we can skip the initial pinging step.

6: Implement Security

Keep your network hardware and infrastructure locked up wherever possible.

The switch for this show is installed in a rack backstage where it's easily accessible by the onstage technicians, but it's in a locked cabinet.

Keep your network off the Internet if possible.

For this simple network, there is no need for an Internet connection. If the console or other gear needs to be updated we can do it in another way.

Use WiFi only if needed, and disable when not in use. Use appropriate WiFi security.

The phone features are only needed during setup and tech time, so the electrician adds powering off the Wireless Access Point to their pre-show check list.

Change default passwords and keep your passwords secure.
The electrician sets a password on the console, and shares it in a secure way with management in case of an emergency.

If using standard computers, install only what is needed for the show on the machine
One of the benefits of using specialized equipment like a lighting console is that it is already optimized for the task and doesn't contain any extraneous stuff on it.

7: Maximize Operational Reliability
What is the backup plan in case of a cable failure?
The electrician has some backup cables ready to go in a closet backstage.

What is the backup plan in case of a network hardware failure?
The electrician wisely bought two show-oriented switches when the system was purchased. One is kept in the backstage workshop for testing and can be quickly swapped out in case of a switch failure.

EXAMPLE SOUND NETWORK

Now let's take a look at a network application for a temporary sound system that is being brought into a venue for a one-off show with an act that needs only a few microphones and has simple performer monitoring needs. We need to connect a digital audio console and its remote control wireless tablet (used to adjust monitors for the performers during sound check), and then also distribute mic inputs from the stage to the console, drive audio from the console to some analog performer monitor speakers, as well as two network-enabled line arrays for the main house system. In addition, a laptop will be connected for playback of audio cues during the show.

1: Analyze Network Needs
What kind of traffic is being carried: Control data and/or media?
This system will need both control (wireless tablet) and streaming media (audio). The main console has two sets of Ethernet jacks; one for the control and the other for the audio transmission network.

Is routing required?
No. Even though we will be running two networks, there's no reason to connect between them.

Does the system need wireless access?
Yes, for the wireless tablet.

What are the network security risks?
This is a sound system that doesn't really present any safety risks to crew or performers, so the only real risk of someone accessing the network is messing with the show. This wouldn't be great, but it's not life or death.

2: Design Address/Subnet Scheme

How many subnets are required?
There are two in this case, running over two virtually separated networks (see below).

How are IP Addresses assigned? (Is a DHCP server needed?)
For control, this sound console uses fixed IP addresses, so those need to be set manually. Link-local (self-assigned) addresses are recommended for the digital audio transmission system, which locates connected devices on any IP address in the same subnet and presents the name of that device for patching. No DHCP server is needed

3: Determine Network Topology

The mixer and the playback laptop will be out in the audience area connected to one switch, while the input/output rack, wireless access point, and a second switch will be on a rack backstage.

Do we need VLANs?
Due to cable run issues (see below) the engineer decides to use shared switches and two VLANs, one for control and one for audio to save on cable runs and switch costs. The control network is only needed during sound check so even if there is a problem it should not affect the show.

Are runs over 100m required in the system?
In this case, because of the physical layout of the venue and numerous aisles that can't be crossed with cable, the run from the Front Of House (FOH) position to backstage is about 400', exceeding the 100 meter (approximately 328 feet) maximum length of Cat 5e. For this reason, the engineer pulls from the rental shop two Ethernet switches designed for entertainment applications that have fiber connections that can run thousands of feet.

Is high bandwidth digital audio or video passing through the network?
While a bunch of channels of audio are needed, the audio networking system used works well on a 1Gbit/s connection, so super high bandwidth is not needed.

Are redundant data pathways required, and if so, how will they be implemented? (STP, EAPS, etc).

The selected switch system offers main and backup fiber connections, which are managed automatically by the switch to avoid broadcast storms.

Are managed and/or multi-layer switches required?

The loop (broadcast storm) management does require a more sophisticated switch, but in this case the show-centric switch chosen has front panel controls and a display that can be used to configure the switch as needed, including assigning specific physical Ethernet interfaces to the appropriate VLAN. So, while switch management is needed, the configuration process has been packaged by the manufacturer to make it very easy to set up the system.

4: Document the Network

IP Address List:

For the fixed IP addresses, the engineer decides to use Class C private ("non-routeable") addresses. The "link-local" addresses will be self-configured by each device in the 169.254.x.x range.

Device	IP Address (Subnet Mask: 255.255.255.0)
Console Control Connection	192.168.101.11
Tablet for Remote Control	192.168.101.12
Console Audio Connection	169.254.x.x (Self-assigned link-local)
Sound Playback System	169.254.x.x (Self-assigned link-local)
Stage Input/Output Box	169.254.x.x (Self-assigned link-local)
Line array L	169.254.x.x (Self-assigned link-local)
Line array R	169.254.x.x (Self-assigned link-local)

Network diagram:

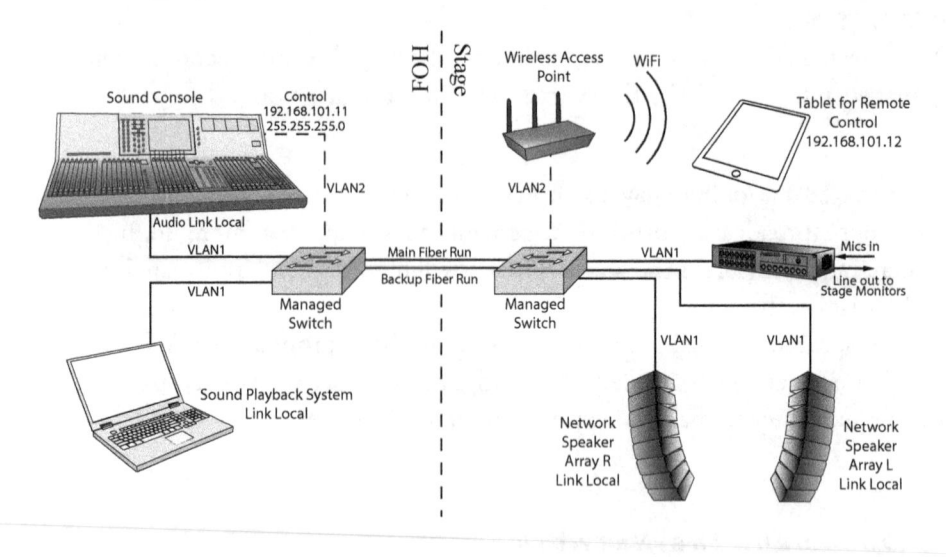

5: Build, Label, and Verify the Network

Double check all cables and labels

The engineer goes through and labels every cable with what it's connected to and where it's going.

Verify IP addresses

The audio networking system has controller software that displays all the connected devices and their IP addresses, so it's very easy to confirm that everything is up and running and connected.

6: Implement Security

Keep your network hardware and infrastructure locked up wherever possible.

The switch for this show is installed in a rack backstage where it's easily accessible by the onstage technicians. However, as a one off show, the primary security mechanism will be the usual backstage security procedures: if someone unknown is observed messing with the switch, it will be pretty obvious and the person can be questioned. A more likely threat is someone spilling a drink into the rack.

Keep your network off the Internet if possible.

For this simple network, there is no need for an Internet connection. If the console or other gear needs to be updated we can do it in another way.

Use WiFi only if needed, and disable when not in use. Use appropriate WiFi security.
The remote tablet features are only needed during sound check, when the engineer will go onstage to adjust the performer monitors. The engineer simply unplugs the Wireless Access Point before the house opens to keep anyone from trying to mess with it.

Change default passwords and keep your passwords secure.
The managed switches do have a password, and the engineer shares it in a secure way with management in case of an emergency.

If using standard computers, install only what is needed for the show on the machine
There is one standard computer for playback on this network, but it's a dedicated playback laptop that has only the playback and minimal other software installed. WiFi is turned off on the laptop.

7: Maximize Operational Reliability
What is the backup plan in case of a cable failure?
The engineer has some backup cables and a spare fiber run ready to go in a road box backstage. In addition, the switch management system will automatically cut over to the backup fiber if one of the FOH/backstage runs gets broken or disconnected.

What is the backup plan in case of a network hardware failure?
The engineer has a spare, configured switch in a road box backstage.

EXAMPLE VIDEO NETWORK

For this example, let's imagine a video system for unattended shows in a small museum. We have a video server that will play back high resolution video to two flat panel video displays, and two projectors. A computer is needed to configure and run the video server, and a show control system will control the scheduling of shows, and also turn the projectors on in the morning and off at the end of the day.

1: Analyze Network Needs
What kind of traffic is being carried: Control data and/or media?
The network solution will need to carry both control and streaming media (video). for which a network based video distribution system has been selected.

Is routing required?
No.

Does the system need wireless access?
No.

What are the network security risks?
This is a video system that doesn't really present any safety risks to crew or performers, so the only real risk of someone accessing the network is messing with the show. This wouldn't be great, but it's not life or death.

2: Design Address/Subnet Scheme

How many subnets are required?
There are two in this case, running over two separated networks, one for control and the other carrying digital video.

How are IP Addresses assigned? (Is a DHCP server needed?)
For control, the system uses fixed IP addresses, so those need to be set manually. This video distribution system uses DHCP addresses, so a DHCP server is available in the 10Gb video distribution switch and that will be used to manage addresses for video distribution.

3: Determine Network Topology

Do we need VLANs?
No.

Are runs over 100m required in the system?
No.

Is high bandwidth digital audio or video passing through the network?
Yes. In this case, high resolution video is needed, which exceeds the capacity of a typical 1 Gbit/s network, so a 10 Gbit/s managed switch designed for show video applications is selected. This switch can either connect via copper cables or fiber.

Are redundant data pathways required, and if so, how will they be implemented? (STP, EAPS, etc).
No.

Are managed and/or multi-layer switches required?
Yes, some features of the video distribution system and the DHCP server need management. The management of the switch is done through a web browser, which can be run on the same computer setup to run the server configuration software.

4: Document the Network
IP Address List:

The installation contractor uses two ranges of Class C private ("non-routeable") IP addresses. The control addresses are manually setup, while the video interfaces are allocated by the DHCP server in a defined range:

Device	IP Address (Subnet Mask: 255.255.255.0)
Computer	192.168.101.11
Show Control	192.168.101.12
Server Control Interface	192.168.101.21
Switch Management Interface	192.168.101.101
Projector 1 Control	192.168.101.31
Projector 2 Control	192.168.101.32
Server Video Interface	192.168.201.x (DHCP)
Video Endpoint 1	192.168.201.x (DHCP)
Video Endpoint 2	192.168.201.x (DHCP)
Projector 1 Video	192.168.201.x (DHCP)
Projector 2 Video	192.168.201.x (DHCP)

Network diagram:

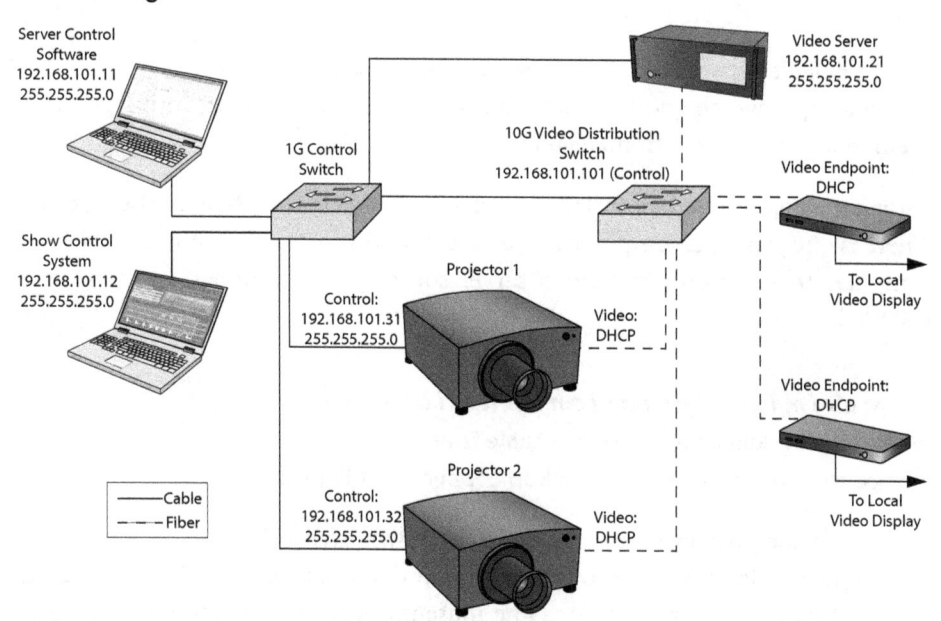

INTRODUCTION TO SHOW NETWORKING • 95

5: Build, Label, and Verify the Network

Double check all cables and labels

The installation contractor goes through and labels every cable with what it's connected to and where it's going.

Verify IP addresses

From the control computer, each device in the control network should be able to be verified using a PING command. The video networking system has management software that displays all the connected devices and their DHCP-assigned IP addresses, so it's very easy to confirm that everything is up and running and connected.

6: Implement Security

Keep your network hardware and infrastructure locked up wherever possible.

The control computer and the switch for this show is installed in a rack in a machine room, which is locked and has limited access. It's possible someone could unplug one of the video devices and plug in a computer, but it would be hard to do anything without the configuration software.

Keep your network off the Internet if possible.

For this simple network, there is no need for an Internet connection.

Use WiFi only if needed, and disable when not in use. Use appropriate WiFi security.

n/a

Change default passwords and keep your passwords secure.

The managed switch and the computer do have password, and contractor shares them in a secure way with management.

If using standard computers, install only what is needed for the show on the machine

There is one standard computer for playback on this network, but it's a dedicated computer that has only the video server software and minimal other software installed.

7: Maximize Operational Reliability

What is the backup plan in case of a cable failure?

The contractor supplies some backup copper and fiber cables.

What is the backup plan in case of a network hardware failure?

The project ended up being over what the museum has budgeted, so there is no spare network or other hardware. The museum hopes to buy more backup gear when funding becomes available.

EXAMPLE SCENERY CONTROL NETWORK

Next let's take a look at a network built for scenic automation, moving two platforms across a stage. The system is made up of a control console (which handles all emergency stop functions independently of the network), a PC for programming and monitoring, a handheld control pendant, and two drive control units. All of the gear is set up backstage, and the control system vendor also supplies an industrial, safety-rated network switch.

1: Analyze Network Needs

What kind of traffic is being carried: Control data and/or media?
This network will be carrying control traffic.

Is routing required?
No.

Does the system need wireless access?
No.

What are the network security risks?
This system can be dangerous to performers and crew, so safety is the top concern, and an attack could be dangerous.

2: Design Address/Subnet Scheme

How many subnets are required?
One

How are IP Addresses assigned? (Is a DHCP server needed?)
This system is based around fixed IP addresses, so those need to be set manually.

3: Determine Network Topology

Do we need VLANs?
No.

Are runs over 100m required in the system?
No.

Is high bandwidth digital audio or video passing through the network?
No.

Are redundant data pathways required, and if so, how will they be implemented?

(STP, EAPS, etc).
No.

Are managed and/or multi-layer switches required?
No, although due to the life-safety implications of the moving scenery, the manufacturer recommends using industrial-grade switches that they recommend.

4: Document the Network
IP Address List:
The automation technician sets up the fixed IP addresses using Class B, private ("non-routeable") addresses.

Device	IP Address (Subnet Mask: 255.255.255.0)
Control Console	172.16.1.101
Programming/Monitoring PC	172.16.1.102
Control Pendant	172.16.1.103
Driver Controller 1	172.16.1.201
Driver Controller 2	172.16.1.202

Network diagram:

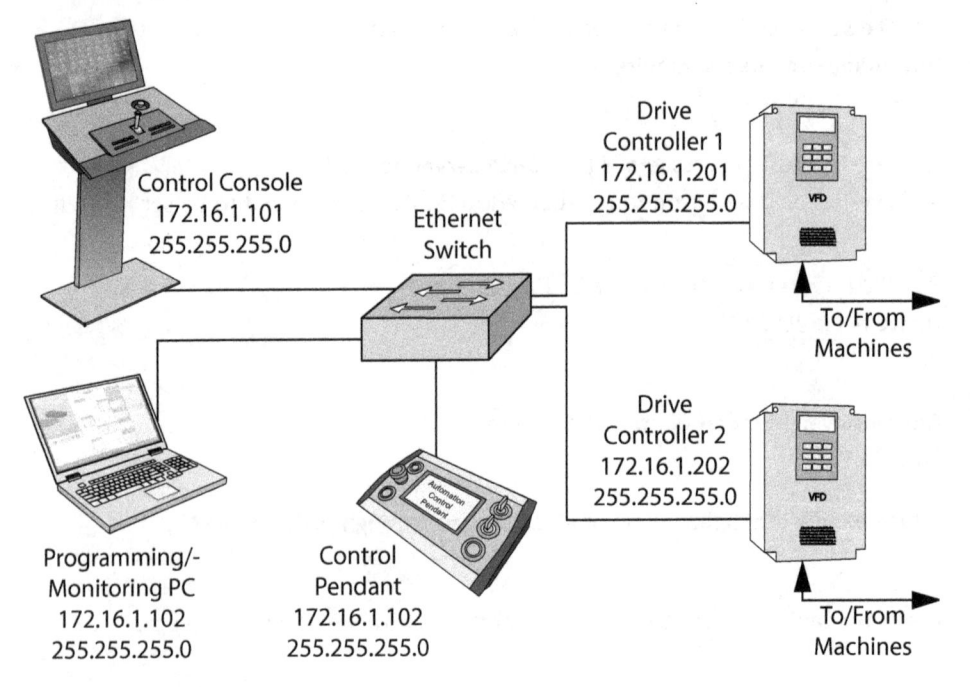

5: Build, Label, and Verify the Network

Double check all cables and labels

The automation technician goes through and labels every cable.

Verify IP addresses

From the control computer, each device in the control network should be able to be verified using a PING command.

6: Implement Security

Keep your network hardware and infrastructure locked up wherever possible.

The operating position onstage is protected by a locked cage, and the network switch is in a rack inside the cage.

Keep your network off the Internet if possible.

There is no need for an Internet connection.

Use WiFi only if needed, and disable when not in use. Use appropriate WiFi security.

One of the reasons no Wi-Fi was include was to minimize the security risk.

Change default passwords and keep your passwords secure.

The controllers all are password protected, and the automation tech shares them in a secure way with management.

If using standard computers, install only what is needed for the show on the machine

There is one standard computer for control on this network, but it's a dedicated computer that has only the control server software and minimal other software installed.

7: Maximize Operational Reliability

What is the backup plan in case of a cable failure?

The system includes backup cables. In addition, heavy duty Ethernet cables and connector shells are used on all cables.

What is the backup plan in case of a network hardware failure?

A spare switch is included in the system in case of a failure.

EXAMPLE MANAGED SHOW CONTROL NETWORK

To bring all this together, let's look at a real managed show network that uses VLANs and routing extensively: our annual *Gravesend Inn*™ interactive haunted hotel themed attraction at New York City College of Technology (Citytech, where I teach). The sprawling, multi-floor walk through attraction with a rich physical scenic environment routinely gets more than 6,000 visitors a year, and it's generally designed to be more fun than scary. There are animatronic characters, animated effects, and of course lighting, sound, and video. What's not obvious (we hope) as you walk through is that the audience members are actually triggering the effects by passing through a number of sensors discreetly positioned throughout. When no one is in the attraction, only the background cues are running; as a group progresses through, each zone is activated, and the audience groups move through like players on a golf course. And one of the unique features of the attraction (spoiler alert!) is that as you go through, you are being watched on surveillance cameras. This might not be surprising, but what is unusual here is that you are being watched by the audience members in front of you who have gone through the attraction. And if you do something entertaining, you might see a replay of yourself on the big screen.[2]

The *Gravesend Inn*™ started in 1999 and was originally built around a hardware-based show control system, with all the sensors and devices connected directly to the unit. Over the years, as we added more and more technology to the attraction, I started moving more and more stuff onto the network, running isolated, physically separated, unmanaged Ethernet switches: one for lighting, one for sound, one for video playback, one for show control, etc. In 2011, I moved the whole thing onto a system of fully managed, layer 3, Gigabit PoE Switches (we need PoE to power video surveillance cameras and other items), and integrated a common physical network infrastructure, using a combination of cables we ran permanently, and temporary runs as well. This network now successfully carries all the lighting, video and show control for the attraction, as well as all the audio and the video from the surveillance camera system. In reality, this network evolved over a decade, but for purposes here let's take a look at my network design process:

1: Analyze Network Needs
What kind of traffic is being carried: Control data and/or media?
This network connects the following control systems:

- Audience Sensors
- Lighting
- Sound Playback
- Video Playback
- Animated Effects

---

[2] If you are in NYC around Halloween come see us!

- Animatronic
- Queue Line Number Display
- Show Controller

Here's a show control block diagram:

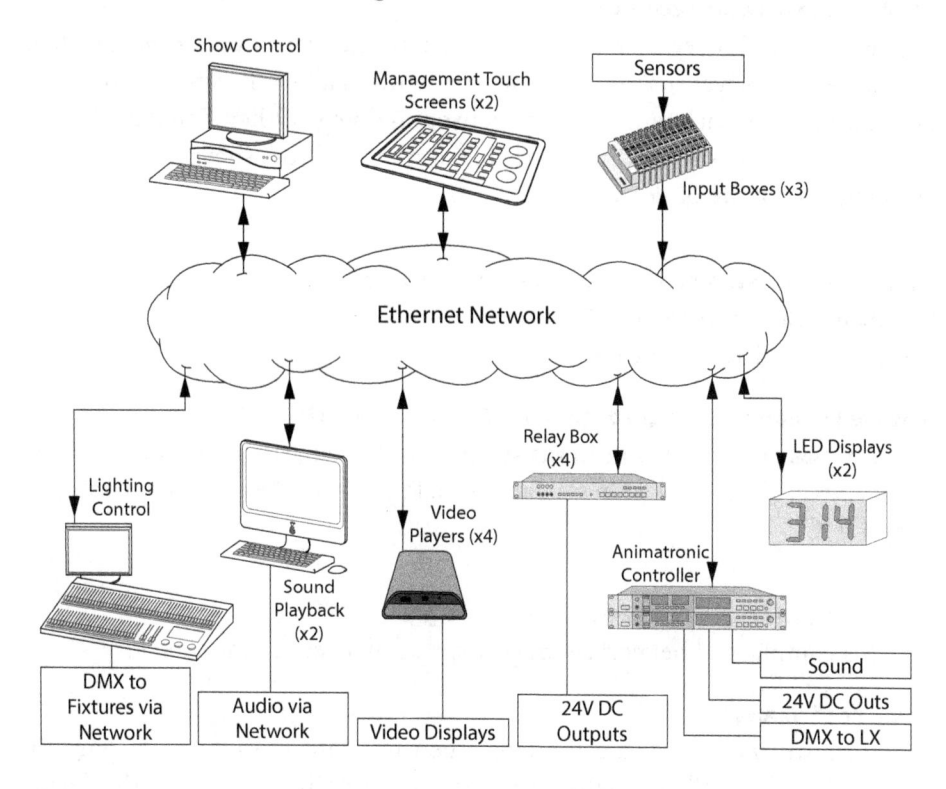

[Diagram: Show control block diagram showing Show Control, Management Touch Screens (x2), Sensors, and Input Boxes (x3) connected via an Ethernet Network cloud. The network also connects to Lighting Control (DMX to Fixtures via Network), Sound Playback (x2) (Audio via Network), Video Players (x4) (Video Displays), Relay Box (x4) (24V DC Outputs), Animatronic Controller (Sound, 24V DC Outs, DMX to LX), and LED Displays (x2).]

In addition, the network connects devices for media distribution:

- Sound
- Surveillance Cameras and Replay

Is routing required?
It would be possible to do this system with a bunch of isolated layer 2 switches, but because the attraction sprawls out over three floors of our building and encompasses our theatre, doing so would make a cable management nightmare (and remember students are building this system). In addition, the show control system needs to talk to every network; that would mean making a bunch of network connections from the show controller out to each entertainment control system network. So, in this case, I decided to go to a routed network so that I could keep

things separated out and still allow the show control access to each of them.

Does the system need wireless access?
Yes, we want wireless access for the programming period.

What are the network security risks?
While some machinery control is run through the network, each of those systems has its own, low-level enabling and safety systems to allow the systems to be shut off regardless of what anything on the network is doing. Other than that, if someone broke into the network they'd be able to mess with the show. Again, it's not great but it's not life or death.

2: Design Address/Subnet Scheme

How many subnets are required?
Several are needed—see below.

How are IP Addresses assigned? (Is a DHCP server needed?)
IP Addresses on control units in the system are manually assigned; connected audio devices use link-local addresses, and the addresses for the cameras are assigned using DHCP.

3: Determine Network Topology

This is a complicated network, with gear spread all over several floors.

Do we need VLANs?
Yes. Here we then subdivide the larger network into 6 VLANs, keeping the streaming media traffic separated from the control traffic. VLAN 1 is the default VLAN to which any unused Ethernet interfaces are assigned; for security reasons it is not used.

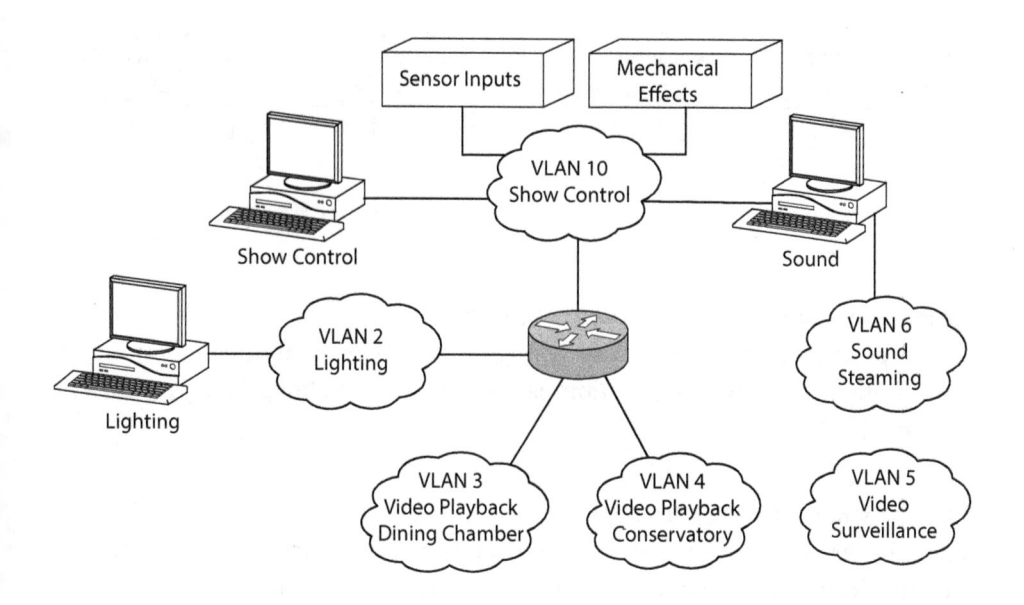

[Diagram: Network topology showing a central router/switch connecting multiple VLANs:
- VLAN 10 Show Control (connected to Sensor Inputs and Mechanical Effects, and Show Control and Sound computers)
- VLAN 2 Lighting (Lighting computer)
- VLAN 6 Sound Steaming
- VLAN 3 Video Playback Dining Chamber
- VLAN 4 Video Playback Conservatory
- VLAN 5 Video Surveillance]

More about the operation of this network in "Explaining The Network" on page 107.

Are runs over 100m required in the system?
No. For this attraction, with so many devices spread across such a large facility, we position four switches throughout our building, and then run cable from each device to the nearest switch, and the longest cable is about 100 feet.

Is high bandwidth digital audio or video passing through the network?
While there are many audio and video devices connected to this network, none of it needs exceptional bandwidth, so a regular 1Gbit/s network is fine.

Are redundant data pathways required, and if so, how will they be implemented? (STP, EAPS, etc).
For this attraction we want a robust system, so a loop makes sense. To keep from causing broadcast storms, we're using a feature of the switches we are using called "Stacking" that implements a RSTP (rapid Spanning Tree Protocol) topology management feature:

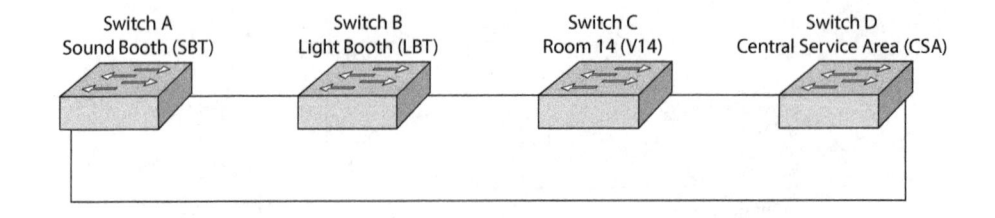

```
Switch A            Switch B            Switch C            Switch D
Sound Booth (SBT)   Light Booth (LBT)   Room 14 (V14)       Central Service Area (CSA)
```

Are managed and/or multi-layer switches required?
Yes. We need the management to configure the VLANs, and also the routing, and set other network configuration parameters (like disabling Energy Efficient Ethernet (EEE).

4: Document the Network

Since this attraction gets assembled and disassembled every year, it's critical to keep the documentation updated, and since this attraction returns year after year, it's also crucial to do complete "as built" documentation.

IP Address List:[3]

Gravesend Inn Network		Subnet Mask:	255.255.255.0
Device	VLAN		IP Address
Show Control/Administration			192.168.10.1
Show Controller	10-ShowControl		192.168.10.11
Attraction Op Touch Screen	10-ShowControl		192.168.10.12
House Mgr Touch Screen	10-ShowControl		192.168.10.13
Network Management Station	10-ShowControl		192.168.10.14
Animatronic Controller	10-ShowControl		192.168.10.21
Animatronic Programming PC	10-ShowControl		192.168.10.21
Sound Playback Control A	10-ShowControl		192.168.10.31
Sound Playback Control B	10-ShowControl		192.168.10.31
Take a Number Sign Lobby	10-ShowControl		192.168.10.41
Take a Number Sign 2nd Floor	10-ShowControl		192.168.10.41
Input Box A	10-ShowControl		192.168.10.101
Input Box B	10-ShowControl		192.168.10.102
Input Box C	10-ShowControl		192.168.10.103

---

3   Not the real IP addresses for security reasons.

Gravesend Inn Network		Subnet Mask:	255.255.255.0
Device	VLAN		IP Address
Relay Box A	10-ShowControl		192.168.10.201
Relay Box B	10-ShowControl		192.168.10.202
Relay Box C	10-ShowControl		192.168.10.203
Relay Box Kitchen Prep	10-ShowControl		192.168.10.204
Lighting			192.168.2.1
Console	2-Lighting		192.168.2.11
Console Backup	2-Lighting		192.168.2.12
DMX Distribution	2-Lighting		192.168.2.13
Console Programming	2-Lighting		192.168.2.14
Wireless Remote	2-Lighting		192.168.2.101
Video Display Dining Chamber			192.168.3.1
Video Player	3-Video DCH		192.168.3.11
Video Display Conservatory			192.168.4.1
Video Player	4-Video CON		192.168.4.11
Video Player	4-Video CON		192.168.4.12
Video Player	4-Video CON		192.168.4.13
Video Surveillance Servers			192.168.5.1
NVR #1	5-Video Surveillance		192.168.5.11
NVR #2	5-Video Surveillance		192.168.5.12
NVR #3	5-Video Surveillance		192.168.5.13
NVR #4	5-Video Surveillance		192.168.5.14
Live Display Machine	5-Video Surveillance		192.168.5.21
Search Client #1	5-Video Surveillance		192.168.5.22
Search Client #2	5-Video Surveillance		192.168.5.23
Projector HL	5-Video Surveillance		192.168.5.31
Projector HR	5-Video Surveillance		192.168.5.32

Gravesend Inn Network		Subnet Mask:	255.255.255.0
Device	VLAN		IP Address
Sound Streaming			192.168.6.1
Sound Playback A Audio Out	6-Sound Streaming		Link Local
Sound Playback B Audio Out	6-Sound Streaming		Link Local
Mixer	6-Sound Streaming		Link Local
8 Channel Audio Input	6-Sound Streaming		Link Local
8 Channel Audio Output	6-Sound Streaming		Link Local
8 Channel Audio Output	6-Sound Streaming		Link Local
8 Channel Audio Input	6-Sound Streaming		Link Local
8 Channel Audio Output	6-Sound Streaming		Link Local
8 Channel Audio Output	6-Sound Streaming		Link Local
8 Channel Audio Output	6-Sound Streaming		Link Local
8 Channel Audio Output	6-Sound Streaming		Link Local

Network diagram:

In this case, the network is too complex to conveniently document with a simple network diagram. The IP address list above, and other paperwork and documentation is what we use to build the network each year.

5: Build, Label, and Verify the Network

Double check all cables and labels

Because there are so many cables on this attraction, we have created an extensive labeling scheme and every single audio, video, show control, and network cable on the attraction is in a database and labels are made for each end of the cable. As soon as each component is brought online we can verify its connection by pinging from the show control or other machine.

Verify IP addresses

For this system, with so many devices needed IP addresses, subnet masks, and default gateways, verifying that what is in the paperwork is correctly entered into the devices is critical.

Ping Everything

One of the first things I do each year as things are connected is ping them. Then connect to them from the show control or other system.

6: Implement Security

Keep your network hardware and infrastructure locked up wherever possible.
Physical security is our first line of defense in this system; all of our network equipment is in controlled (and surveilled) areas where it would be very obvious if an intruder was attempting to connect to the network.

Keep your network off the Internet if possible.
This system is not connected to the Internet at all. If remote access were needed, we would establish a single computer for access, that sits on two networks: the public facing Internet, and another interface into the show system. We would then use secure remote access protocols and techniques to ensure extremely limited and monitored access to that computer.

Use WiFi only if needed, and disable when not in use. Use appropriate WiFi security.
WiFi access is disabled after programming is complete and before the audience comes in.

Change default passwords and keep your passwords secure.
Passwords are changed each year and tightly controlled.

If using standard computers, install only what is needed for the show on the machine
This system is made up of many standard computers, but we strive to keep them as stripped down and controlled as possible.

7: Maximize Operational Reliability

What is the backup plan in case of a cable failure?
We have many spare cables. If there is a failure in this system, we can either hold the audience line or shut down briefly to make repairs.

What is the backup plan in case of a network hardware failure?
We have an extra switch configured and ready to go, and documented procedures to switch it out.

Explaining The Network

This is a complicated but powerful network; let's talk through its operation to illustrate the concepts we've been covering in this book.

VLANs/Subnets

While the entire network shares a common physical infrastructure, each of the VLANs is—effectively—a separate virtual network. The six VLANs are configured into the switch system using its Web-based management interface (I keep extensive documentation on this process so students can easily recreate it each year), and physical Ethernet interfaces on each of the four switches are assigned to a particular VLAN though a simple web-based operation. Each VLAN is allocated to a particular purpose; let's go through each one.

The lighting VLAN services the lighting console, a backup console, a network processing unit that distributes DMX, and two wireless access points for programming (one in our theatre and one in the basement; these are disabled after technical rehearsals for security reasons). All the Ethernet switch interfaces used by these devices are assigned to VLAN 2, and work on a subnet of `192.168.2.0`, with a subnet mask of `255.255.255.0 (/24)`.

Sound effects for the show come from two computers running sound effects playback software, which distribute dozens of channels of digital audio over a network audio interface, connected through VLAN 6. This audio network includes a high level process that discovers IP addresses (as long as they are in the same subnet) so while I reserved the `192.168.6.0/24` subnet, the devices in this VLAN actually use self-assigned link-local addresses. With this VLAN heavily loaded with dozens of channels of streaming, high sample rate digital audio, I wanted to keep the control signals firing the actual cues separate. So how do I fire sound cues from show control?

Take a look at the system diagram again and you will see *two* lines leading out from the sound effects playback computers; one of those goes to the audio streaming network (VLAN 6); the other goes to show control (VLAN 10). To make this work, we used both Ethernet interfaces included on the sound effects machine with two physical Ethernet interfaces[4]; one resides on the sound streaming VLAN; the other resides on the show control VLAN in the `192.168.10.0/24` main show control subnet. The sound effects computer operating system internally sends its packets to the proper interface based on each packet's IP address; audio samples flow out on the interface connected to the sound subnet, while control messages come and go on the main show control network interface.

Video playback for the attraction is done using network controllable hardware video servers that read off an internal memory card and output digital video to a local monitor; these devices use a proprietary protocol to synchronize multiple video displays on the network. To keep these two systems separated (for ease of programming and control) I used two VLANs. VLAN 3 and subnet

---

4 It would likely be possible to combine these two networks, but I like the redundancy offered by two separate physical connections.

192.168.3.0/24 is for a single "dining chamber" video server; VLAN 4 and subnet 192.168.4.0/24 is for a three-screen bay window effect.

Next up is the video surveillance system which, with numerous IP Power over Ethernet (PoE) cameras, generates an enormous amount of streaming traffic from the cameras to commercial, security-grade Network Video Recorder (NVR) servers. The cameras, of course, were spread all over the attraction and simply connected via whichever of the four NVRs was physically closest; the NVR also contains a DHCP server to assign addresses to the local cameras. The NVRs are then connected to the main network, and stream out multi-camera live view and instant replays via some standard PCs.

Layer 3 Routing

I've skimmed over one important VLAN: VLAN 10, which contains the computer running the show control system, the animatronic and other controllers, multiple input boxes that read in sensor status from all over the attraction, output relay boxes that control the animated effects throughout the attraction, and other control-related devices. In addition to these sensors, actuators, and similar devices, the show control system also needs to communicate with and control other all the systems—lighting, sound, and video—which all reside on different VLANs. How can they communicate? We use inter-VLAN routing.

To see how this works, let's say we try to send a "play" command from the show control system at 192.168.10.11 to the video display server at 192.168.3.11. These systems are on different subnets (192.168.10.0/24 and 192.168.4.0/24) and different VLANs, and can not see each other or connect. The managed switches we use have some Layer 3 capabilities, meaning that they can understand not only the raw layer 2 Ethernet addresses of each frame, but also the associated IP addresses of the packets. So, the "stacked" system as a whole offers a feature that (when enabled) implements a router that can pass traffic back and forth between the VLANs. This feature very easy to use—you just enable the feature and when the switch system sees IP traffic on a particular VLAN, it automatically creates a routing table entry to forward packets to the correct destination on each VLAN.

For this to work, each machine on the network needs, in addition to an IP address and subnet mask, to have a properly configured default gateway. In the simple (but more than adequate) routing in this switch system, you assign an IP address like 192.168.10.1 to VLAN 10; that then becomes the default gateway. For example, the video playback systems on VLAN 3, which have addresses in the 192.168.3.0 network, is configured with a default gateway of 192.168.3.1.

All the devices in the show control VLAN 10/`192.168.10.0` subnet are configured with a default gateway of `192.168.10.1`, and so on. In this way, the host can properly send packets to the correct gateway, and then the router can correctly forward packets between the VLANs.

In the end, this integrated network approach worked really well for us, but it would certainly be just as effective to build the system using multiple unmanaged switches, one for each network. The network has worked reliably for a decade now, and I encourage you to come see it in action!

CONCLUSION

Many aspects of the late 1980s entertainment control world in which I started my career are gone. Back then, most shows used simple control protocols to link a few devices; more complex, powerful systems had to be custom engineered, and this meant that these technologies were available in limited ways only to theme parks and other shows and attractions with larger budgets and resources. I'm not a nostalgic person, and so I say good riddance to the old days. The victory of Ethernet over its contenders, coupled with amazing computer power, has now leveled the playing field, distributing these amazing control technologies to ever-smaller kinds of production. Little low-budget productions here in New York these days have creation power and interaction capabilities in a laptop that would have only been available to theme park designers in the 1990s. I have also argued[1] that the technology is stabilizing and maturing, and this is a good thing, since it allows us to focus more on doing shows instead of inventing tools. I would also argue that we are no longer significantly restricted by technology, but instead are only limited by the laws of nature, budget and our creative imaginations. This is something I couldn't have written in my first book in 1994.

Even though I'm writing this in the middle of an unprecedented pandemic that has (temporarily, I believe) devastated our industry, the future for live shows seems very bright to me. The human need to be together in one place and share stories and experiences is deep, and shows are something I miss deeply and can't wait to do again.

CONTACT INFO AND BLOG

If you have any comments, questions, or corrections, I'd like to hear them. Please check my website at: http://www.controlgeek.net You can contact me from there, and I have a blog, book errata, and video lectures.

Thanks! John Huntington, Brooklyn, NYC

---

[1] See the articles I wrote here https://controlgeek.net/blog/2020/8/20/development-and-evolution-of-show-technology-articles-and-timeline

APPENDIX: NUMBERING SYSTEMS

If—like me—you struggle with math, this section might seem intimidating. However, it's really simple arithmetic, and so it's not that bad. And most of all this topic is important because while we interface with the systems described in this book as humans, the machines only operate in binary. Understanding the internal language of the network makes it a lot easier to deal with things like IP addresses and subnet masks.

BASE 10 (DECIMAL) NOTATION

Humans generally deal with quantities in **base 10,** where numerals represent quantities of ones, tens, hundreds, thousands, and so on.[1] Numbers in base 10 are represented with the "Arabic" digits 0 through 9; in base 10, the symbols "235" represent a quantity of two hundred and thirty-five units. Each position in the numeral 235 has a certain "weight." The least significant (rightmost) digit (5) has a weight of 1, or 10^0; the most significant (leftmost) digit (2) has a weight of 100, or 10^2.

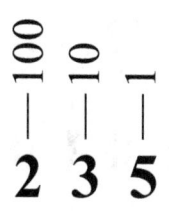

$$\begin{array}{ccc} 100 & 10 & 1 \\ | & | & | \\ 2 & 3 & 5 \end{array}$$

---

1 Why base 10? Ask evolution and count your fingers.

The numeral 235 breaks down as follows (right to left, or least to most significant digit):

Symbol	Weight	Quantity	Total
5	$10^0 = 1$	5×1	5
3	$10^1 = 10$	3×10	30
2	$10^2 = 100$	2×100	200
			235

BASE 2 (BINARY) NOTATION

While humans deal intuitively with base 10, digital machines operate natively in a **binary**, or **base two**, universe. At the lowest level, they deal with only two states: on or off.

Correspondingly, when base 2 is represented using Arabic numerals, only the first two digits are used: 0 and 1.

In a digital system, each digit of a binary number is called a **"bit,"** which is short for binary digit. A bit is simply an on or off state (1 or 0), referenced to a specific point in time. Since a single bit can represent only two possible quantities (one or none), bits are generally grouped into "words." The most common word size is a group of eight bits called a **byte** or, more accurately, an **octet**.[2] A part of a byte (usually four bits) is sometimes called a **nibble**.

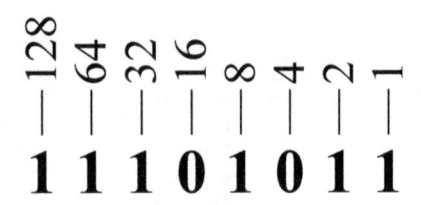

```
128 64 32 16  8  4  2  1
 |   |  |  |  |  |  |  |
 1   1  1  0  1  0  1  1
```

The bits in an octet are numbered 0–7 (right to left), with the bit position num-

---

2 The term "byte" is sometimes (and somewhat incorrectly) used to refer to a word containing any number of bits; the term "octet" is more specific, and refers only to eight-bit words. For this reason, you will find it used in many network standards.

bers corresponding to the digit's weight. An octet can represent 256 different quantities (0–255). As in base 10, the least significant (rightmost) binary digit represents single units: in base 2, this digit can denote only 0 or 1. Weights in binary numbers are powers of 2, so the next digit to the left, or the next most significant digit, represents the quantity of twos, the next the quantity of fours, the next the quantity of eights, and so on.

The quantity of 235 units has a binary equivalent of 11101011, which breaks down into base 10 as follows (right to left, or least to most significant digit):

Symbol	*Weight*	*Quantity*	*Total*
1	$2^0 = 1$	1×1	1
1	$2^1 = 2$	1×2	2
0	$2^2 = 4$	0×4	0
1	$2^3 = 8$	1×8	8
0	$2^4 = 16$	0×16	0
1	$2^5 = 32$	1×32	32
1	$2^6 = 64$	1×64	64
1	$2^7 = 128$	1×128	128
			235

BASE 16 (HEXADECIMAL) NOTATION

Since humans work primarily in base 10, and computers use base 2, you may be wondering why we are covering **base 16**, or **hexadecimal** ("hex"). The reason is that hex is very useful as an alternative (and much easier) way to deal with the eight-bit binary number groupings found so commonly in computing and networking, because each binary nibble (four bits) can range in value from 0 to 15 decimal (one digit in hex) and, therefore, an octet can easily be represented by two hex digits.

Since there are only ten symbols in the Arabic number system, the digits 0–9 are used to represent hex values 0–9, and the letters A–F are used to represent hex values 10–15:

Decimal Digit	Hex Digit
0	0
1	1
2	2
3	3
4	4
5	5
6	6
7	7
8	8
9	9
10	A
11	B
12	C
13	D
14	E
15	F

In hex, the least significant digit represents (as is the case with all the other bases) the quantity of ones (16^0). The next most significant digit represents counts of 16 (16^1), and so on.

$$\underset{\textbf{E}}{\underset{|}{16}}\,\underset{\textbf{B}}{\underset{|}{1}}$$

So the decimal quantity 235 is EB in hex, and breaks down as follows:

Symbol	Weight	Quantity	Total
B	$16^0 = 1$	11×1	11
E	$16^1 = 16$	14×16	224
			235

To further clarify, here are a few examples of some hex numbers and their decimal equivalents:

Decimal	Hex
000	00
001	01
015	0F
016	10
127	7F
255	FF
256	100
512	200
4095	FFF

NUMBER CONTEXT

A number like 1001000 could be representing a quantity in binary, hex, or decimal (or any other related base), so it's important to know the context of the number you're looking at. In programming, you may also see a notation like 0x preceding a hex number, or you may see an upper- or lower-case "h" (h or H) appended to the number. But they all mean the same thing: the number is hexadecimal.

CONVERTING NUMBER BASES

Converting numbers between bases is not something you need to do routinely; most computer operating systems have built-in calculators that make this easy. However, it's helpful to understand how conversion between bases is done, so let's work through several examples.

Binary to Hex

Creating hex numbers from binary is quite simple. First determine the value represented by the least significant nibble, and write the hex symbol denoting that value (0–F$_{16}$). Next, determine the value of the most significant nibble and write that hex symbol to the left of the character you just wrote. For example, let's figure out the hex equivalent of the binary number 11101011. First break the octet into two nibbles:

Least significant nibble: 1011

Most significant nibble: 1110

Working through the bits of the least significant nibble from right to left (least significant bit to most significant bit), 1011 has a value of 1 ones, 1 two, 0 fours, and 1 eight; 1 + 2 + 0 + 8 = 11 (decimal). The symbol representing 11 in hex is B. Now let's analyze the most significant nibble, 1110. It has a value of 8 + 4 + 2 + 0 = 14, or E in hex. So the hex representation of 11101011 is EB$_{16}$—our old friend 235.

Hex to Binary

What do we do if we want to convert hexadecimal numbers into binary? You can easily work through the process detailed above in reverse. However, for purposes of understanding, let's work through a conversion to base 10 first. Let's try the hex number D4$_{16}$:

Symbol	Weight	Quantity	Total
4	16^0 = 1	4 × 1	4
D	16^1 = 16	13 × 16	208
			212

Decimal to Binary

Now, let's convert the decimal number 212 into binary. First, let's determine if an eight-bit word can represent a number as big as 212. What is the biggest binary number we can represent with eight bits (11111111)? Math tells us that it is $2^n - 1$, where n is the number of bits.[3]

But let's look at that in a more intuitive way:

---

[3] We subtract one because 0 is a valid value. For example, 2^8 would be 256, so an octet can represent 256 possible values. But since 0 is a valid value, the highest decimal value that can be represented by eight bits is 256 − 1, or 255.

Symbol	Weight	Quantity	Total
1	$2^0 = 1$	1×1	1
1	$2^1 = 2$	1×2	2
1	$2^2 = 4$	1×4	4
1	$2^3 = 8$	1×8	8
1	$2^4 = 16$	1×16	16
1	$2^5 = 32$	1×32	32
1	$2^6 = 64$	1×64	64
1	$2^7 = 128$	1×128	128
			255

The table shows that an octet can represent any decimal number up to 255, which is bigger than the 212 we're trying to convert. So, to make the conversion, we'll simply subtract out the biggest number possible, and proceed until there is nothing left from the subtraction.

First, let's determine the quantity represented by the most significant binary digit in our decimal number 212. In this case, we're dealing with an octet, so the most significant digit has a weight of 128, and we can either have one or zero 128s. Since 128 (2^7) is less than 212, we'll subtract, and then progress through each binary digit.

$$\begin{array}{r} 212 \\ -128 \ (2^7) \\ \hline 84 \end{array}$$

We now know that the most significant bit will be a one, but we don't know the value of the other bits. So this gives us 1???????, and we can move on.

$$\begin{array}{r} 84 \\ -64 \ (2^6) \\ \hline 20 \end{array}$$

This gives us 11??????. Now let's try the next most significant digit.

$$\begin{array}{r} 20 \\ -32 \ (2^5) \\ \hline ?? \end{array}$$

Twenty, our remainder, is smaller than 32. So what quantity of 32s can we use to represent it? Zero. So this gives us `110?????`, and now we can try the next most significant digit.

$$\begin{array}{r} 20 \\ -16 \ (2^4) \\ \hline 4 \end{array}$$

We can subtract a quantity of one 16, giving us a remainder of four. So we now have `1101????`, and now we can move on to the next most significant digit.

$$\begin{array}{r} 4 \\ -8 \ (2^3) \\ \hline ? \end{array}$$

Eight is bigger than four, so we get zero eights, and we now have `11010???`.

$$\begin{array}{r} 4 \\ -4 \ (2^2) \\ \hline 0 \end{array}$$

Subtracting 1 fours digit, we get `110101??`. Since we have zero left over, we don't need to do any more subtraction, and we can fill in the rest of the number with zeroes, giving us `11010100`.

So, we converted our hexadecimal number D4 into the decimal number 212, and that decimal number into the binary `11010100`.

SAMPLE NUMBERS IN DIFFERENT FORMATS

Just to review, the table below shows some examples of the same number represented in different number schemes.

Decimal	*Binary*	*Hex*
000	00000000	00
001	00000001	01
015	00001111	0F
016	00010000	10
020	00010100	14

033	00100001	21
070	01000110	46
085	01010101	55
127	01111111	7F
128	10000000	80
137	10001001	89
175	10101111	AF
219	11011011	DB
231	11100111	E7
240	11110000	F0
255	11111111	FF

INDEX

SYMBOLS
2.5GBASE-T 24
5GBASE-T 24
8P8C 11
10BASE-T 25
10 Gigabit Ethernet 24
100BASE-T 24
802.3at 29
802.3bt 29
1000BASE-T 24

A
Address Resolution Protocol (ARP) 50, 56
AES-67 3
AES-70 (Open Control Architecture) 3
American Standard Code for Information Interchange (ASCII) 7
APIPA, see Automatic Private IP Addressing
application layer 16
ARP cache 51
ARP command 62
ARP request 51
ARP, See Address Resolution Protocol
ARP table 52
Art-Net 2
ASCII, See American Standard Code for Information Interchange
Audinate Dante 3
auto-IP 41
Automatic Private IP Addressing (APIPA) 40
auto-MDIX 26
AVB 3, 78

B
balanced transmission 11
bandwidth 6
base 2 116
base 10 115
base 16 117
binary xv, 116

binary digit 116
bit 116
bit rate 6
bits per second (BPS) 6
bitwise AND 43
Blair, Scott 77
Bollinger, Aaron xvi
BPS, see bits per second
bridge 29, 30
broadcast 9, 51
broadcast domain 63
broadcast IP address 38, 39
broadcast storm 66
byte 116

C

Carrier Sense, Multiple Access (CSMA) 22
Cat 5e, see Category 5e
Category 5e 10, 78
Category 6 10, 78
Category 6A 11, 78
CIDR, see Classless Inter-Domain Routing
Citytech 99
Classless Inter-Domain Routing (CIDR) 38
CLI, see Command Line Interface
collision detection 22
colon-hexadecimal 54
command line interface (CLI) 28
common carrier 6
concerts xiv
connection-oriented 36
Control Systems for Live Entertainment xiii
corporate event xiv
crimping 12
crossover 25
cruise ship xiv
CSMA, see Carrier Sense Multiple Access
Cyclic Redundancy Check (CRC) 8

D

Dante, see Audinate Dante 3
data collision 22
datagrams 36
default gateway 39, 73
default VLAN 102
deterministic 7
DHCP Reservation 40

DHCP, see Dynamic Host Configuration Protocol
DHCP server 39, 79
differential 11
digital 1
direct connection cable 25
DMX512-A 2
DNS, see Domain Name System
Domain Name System (DNS) 56, 75
dot-decimal 37, 53
Dynamic Host Configuration Protocol (DHCP) 39, 56

E

EAPS, see Ethernet Automatic Protection Switching (EAPS)
EEE, see Energy-Efficient Ethernet
electrical isolation 23
encapsulated 16
Energy-Efficient Ethernet (EEE) 28, 78
entertainment control xiii
entertainment control systems xiii, 5
entertainment technology xv
error detection 8
Ethercon 12
Ethernet xiii, xiv, 1, 21
Ethernet Automatic Protection Switching (EAPS) 67

F

fiber-optic cable 14
fiber, single mode 79
filter 27, 65
fixed IP addresses 41
flood 75
flooding 27, 65
forwarding 27, 65
fountain xiv
frame check sequence 23
frames 8
full-duplex 27

G

gateway 2
global unicast 55
gratuitous ARP 51
Gravesend Inn 99
Gross, Kevin 77

H

hardware address 50
hexadecimal 117
hex, see hexadecimal
host 1
hub 26, 59, 60

I

IEEE 802.1Q 72
IEEE 802.3af Power over Ethernet (PoE) 29
IEEE 802.3 Ethernet Working Group 21
IEEE 802.11 "Wi-Fi" 15, 30, 79
IEEE, see Institute of Electrical and Electronics Engineers
ifconfig 41
IGMP, see Internet Group Management Protocol (IGMP)
IGMP Snooping 75
industrial-grade switches 98
Institute of Electrical and Electronics Engineers (IEEE) 21
Internet 6
Internet Group Management Protocol (IGMP) 38, 75, 78
Internet Protocol (IP) 6, 18, 35, 36, 39
Internet Protocol Version 4 (IPv4) 53
Internet Protocol version 6 (IPv6) 53
IP address 36, 39
ipconfig 41
IP, see Internet Protocol

L

LAN, see Local Area Network
lasers xiii
latency 7
layer 15
layered communications system 15
LC-duplex connector 15, 79
life-safety 98
line-rate 28
Link Layer Discovery Protocol (LLDP) 76
link-local 40, 55
LLC, see Logical Link Control
LLDP, see Link Layer Discovery Protocol 76
Local Area Network (LAN) 5, 6
local host 38
Loewen, Kevin 77
Logical Link Control (LLC) 21
loopback 38

M

MAC address 22, 52

MAC, see Media Access Control
magic 7
managed switch 28
Mbit/s 6
Media Access Control (MAC) 21
MIDI, see Musical Instrument Digital Interface
midspan 30
Milan 3, 78
ModBusTCP 4
multicasting 9, 38, 75
multilayer switch 28
multi-mode fiber 14
museum xiv
Musical Instrument Digital Inteface (MIDI) 3

N

native VLAN 72
NDP, see Neighbor Discovery Protocol 56
Neighbor Discovery Protocol (NDP)
network 1
network address 39
network identifier 37, 39
Network Interface Controller (NIC) 23, 25
New York City College of Technology 99
nibble 116
NIC, see Network Interface Controller
node 1, 25
nonroutable 39
North American Theater Engineering and Architecture Conference (NATEAC) 77

O

octet 37, 116
Open Sound Control (OSC) 3
Open Systems Interconnection (OSI) 17
optical fiber 14
Organizationally Unique Identifier (OUI) 23
OSC, see Open Sound Control
OSI, see Open Systems Interconnection
OUI, see Organizationally Unique Identifier

P

packets 8
phantom power 29, 30
PHY, see Physical Layer
physical address 23
physical layer (PHY) 21, 23
ping 42

plenum 12
PoE, see Power over Ethernet
point-to-point 1
ports 52
Power over Ethernet (PoE) 78, 109
prefix 54
private networking 39
pyro xiii

Q
QoS, see Quality of Service
Quality of Service (QoS) 76

R
Rapid Spanning Tree Protocol (RSTP) 67, 103
RDMnet 2
RDM, see Remote Device Management
registered jack 11
reliable 36
Remote Device Management (RDM) 2
RF 30
RJ45 (8P8C) 11, 13
router 28, 59, 75
router address 73
routing 109
routing table 73
RSTP, see Rapid Spanning Tree Protocol

S
sACN, see streaming ACN
SDVoE, see Software Defined Video over Ethernet
serial 1, 2
Service Set IDentifier (SSID) 31
session 18
SFP, SFP+ see Small Form factor Pluggable
show control xiii, 5
show must go on 83
Show Networks and Control Systems xiii
show system design principles 83
Small Form factor Pluggable (SFP), (SFP+) 15, 79
SMPTE2110 3
socket 52
Software Defined Video over Ethernet (SDVoE) 3
solid conductors 11
Spanning Tree Protocol (STP) 67
SSID, see Service Set IDentifier
stateless address autoconfiguration 40

static IP address 41
Stepniewicz, Peter 77
STP, see twisted pair, shielded, or Spanning Tree Protocol
stranded cables 11
streaming xv, 1
streaming ACN (sACN) 2
subnet mask 43
subnets 43
switches 27, 59
switching fabric 28
switching hubs 27

T
T568A 13
T568B 13
tagging 72
TCP, see Transmission Control Protocol
TIA-568 12
Time Sensitive Networking (TSN) 3, 78
Transmission Control Protocol (TCP) 35
TSN, see Time Sensitive Networking
twisted pair, shielded (STP) 11, 78
twisted pair, unshielded (UTP) 11

U
UDP, see User Datagram Protocol
ULA, see Unique Local Addresses
unicast 9, 60
Unicode 7, 8
Unique Local Addresses (ULA) 55
unmanaged switches 28
unreliable 36
User Datagram Protocol (UDP) 35, 36
UTF-8 7
UTP, see twisted pair, unshielded

V
virtual circuit 36
Virtual Local Area Network (VLAN) 70, 78, 99, 109
Virtual Private Network (VPN) 76, 79
VLAN, see Virtual Local Area Network
VLAN trunk 72
VPN, see Virtual Private Network

W
WAN, see Wide Area Network

Wide Area Network (WAN) 5, 6
Wi-Fi, see IEEE 802.11 "Wi-Fi"
Wireless Access Point (WAP) 30
WireShark 39

Z
Zircon Designs Press ii

CPSIA information can be obtained
at www.ICGtesting.com
Printed in the USA
BVHW092205200521
607797BV00005B/781

9 781735 763804